A NAFTA GUIDEBOOK FOR NORTH AMERICAN TRUCKERS

Trucking Guide to Border Crossing

ALICE ADAMS

THOMSON

DELMAR LEARNING

Australia Canada Mexico Singapore Spain United Kingdom United States

THOMSON

DELMAR LEARNING

Trucking Guide to Border Crossing
A NAFTA Guidebook for North American Truckers
Alice Adams

Vice President,
Technology and Trades
SBU:
Alar Elken

Executive Director,
Professional Business Unit:
Gregory L. Clayton

Editorial Director:
Sandy Clark

Product Development
Manager:
Timothy Waters

Development Editor:
Angie Khong Davis

Marketing Director:
Beth A. Lutz

Marketing Specialist:
Brian McGrath

Production Director:
Mary Ellen Black

Production Manager:
Larry Main

Production Editor:
Sharon Popson

Editorial Assistant:
Kristen Shenfield

NOTICE TO THE READER

Contents

Preface

Trucking Guide to Border Crossing: A NAFTA Guidebook for North American Truckers is one of the first practical and down-to-earth guides for professional drivers crossing borders between Canada, the United States, and Mexico. Written in an easily readable style and providing explanations for many of the terms relative to policies and paperwork required among the three countries, *Border Crossing* will remove many of the "surprises" truckers may encounter when doing business in Canada, the United States, and Mexico. It untangles much of the red tape involved in the transportation of goods across these countries' borders and, on the lighter side, offers a "tourist's" view for those entering a "foreign country" for the first time, including information regarding speed limits, firearms laws, and alcoholic beverages, as well as other "must-know" facts about each country. *Border Crossing* is designed with extensive and detailed information that will make every driver using the book an asset to international carriers and their clients.

About the Author

Alice Adams is an educator and veteran transportation writer for *The Houston Chronicle*, and national transportation trade publications. After serving in academic positions at Odessa College (Texas) and The University of St. Thomas, she has authored several transportation industry books, including texts used in public, private, and proprietary professional driving schools. Her other books include *A Survival Guide for Truck Drivers: Tips from the Trenches*, *Pass the CDL: Everything You Need to Know*, and *Trucking Rules and Regulations: A Reference Guide to Transportation Industry Regulations*, all published by Delmar Learning. She has been named to the Who's Who in International Writers, Outstanding Young Professional Women, and Top Professional Women in Texas.

Acknowledgments

This book is written as a team effort with some of the best in the business. Truckloads of thanks go to my editor, Angie Davis, who has the eye of an eagle, the patience of Job, and an unfailing sense of humor. Much of the credit for this book and the fulfillment of its mission also goes to the tireless research efforts of Kristin Berthelsen, and the experience and contributions of Ron Adams, who has driven thousands of miles in each of the three NAFTA nations.

Introduction

Photo courtesy of Erik Berthelsen.

WHY THIS GUIDEBOOK WAS WRITTEN AND HOW TO USE IT

Beginning in 1992, NAFTA—the North American Free Trade Agreement—became a household word across North America, discussed and re-discussed in newspapers, reported on television, and addressed as a priority topic at most industry conventions.

Although it had been the topic of international debate for many years and by several presidents, NAFTA emerged as a reality with its first drafts in 1992.

NAFTA's goals were simple—to open trade opportunities among three neighboring nations in North America—Canada, the United States, and Mexico.

What this meant to trucking companies and truck drivers was an opportunity to pick up and deliver loads across borders, much the same as they had always done in their own states, provinces, and communities.

Today, there are still points of NAFTA under discussion, but once those controversies are resolved, it will be feasible for a truck from Mexico to travel in the United States, delivering Mexican shipments and picking up loads going to Mexico or Canada before returning home to Mexico.

The information provided here for professional drivers will make it possible for drivers to enter another country well-equipped with information about how to do his or her job—and without breaking any laws or putting themselves in harm's way.

As professionals, truckers are accountable for knowing the traffic laws and various requirements of each country. This guidebooks enhances that accountability by providing laws, customs, and other "need-to-know" information while driving in any of the countries involved in NAFTA.

If, for example, a United States-based driver is called upon to deliver a load in Canada, a quick scan of this book, and particularly the chapter on "Crossing into Canada," will make the laws easier to understand and will point out any differences in traffic laws or road rules for that country.

There are also several appendices included at the back of this book. Use these resources to learn more about the customs and backgrounds of the countries you are in, when you have questions about traffic signage, or need to learn simple phrases to use when dealing with non-English speakers.

CHAPTER 1

NAFTA 101

"Here it is!
Part 95 of section 33 of Article L of NAFTA clearly states . . . "

Cartoon by T. McCracken.

WHAT TRUCK DRIVERS NEED TO KNOW ABOUT NAFTA

Reading the full NAFTA text would probably require training in international trade as well as international law. So what do drivers basically need to know about NAFTA?

Along with the rest of the transportation industry, most drivers have had many opportunities to become acquainted with the big picture of NAFTA, through the newspaper, truck stop discussions, or osmosis while listening to the nightly news.

Some drivers have feared that NAFTA would put them out of work. As of 2003, there are driver shortages in all three NAFTA countries, so loss of work is not a major issue. Other drivers have seen NAFTA as an opportunity to work . . . even offering employment security.

When it was implemented in January 1994, NAFTA's originators intended to improve all facets of doing business among the participating countries—Canada, the United States, and Mexico. Their goal was to eliminate almost all tariffs between the United States and Mexico by 2008 and the tariffs between the United States and Canada by 1998. The original drafters of the agreement also targeted the barriers to trade—such as import licenses—that would exclude a specific country's products from any of the participating countries.

At this writing (Fall, 2003), trucks from Mexico continue to be held at the border into the United States and United States trucks cannot service Mexico. Talks continue to move forward but no trucks from Mexico can exceed the 20-mile limit in the United States. The same applies to United States trucks going into Mexico.

As originally written, NAFTA set dates where transportation of international goods and people could begin crossing borders. For trucks and buses, NAFTA was written to allow motor carriers to do business on both sides of all borders on a phased schedule over six years—beginning in 1995. The United States, however, continues to postpone full implementation of NAFTA due to public concerns regarding safety and pressures from a variety of United States-based special interest groups.

A special NAFTA panel ruled that United States refusal to recognize applications for operating authority by Mexican carriers in the United States violated the NAFTA agreement. Since that time, the Department of Transportation Appropriations Act for fiscal year 2002 was passed, establishing the requirements for application procedures and operations of Mexican trucking firms in the United States, effective May 2002.

On June 5, 2001, President George W. Bush removed restrictions so that Mexican citizens could establish companies in the United States to (1) transport international cargo between points in the United States or (2) transport passengers between points in the United States. If you notice traffic on major interstate highways, you'll see a definite increase in Mexican bus traffic.

On November 27, 2002, President Bush also removed cross-border access restrictions to permit qualified Mexico-based motor carriers to have operating authority in the United States, either to transport passengers in cross-border scheduled buses or to provide cross-border transportation services for international goods. However, Mexican trucks continue to be banned from United States highways.

All motor carriers operating in NAFTA countries must follow the same federal and state/provincial regulations and procedures that apply to all carriers originating in that country. All safety regulations, insurance requirements, tariff requirements, and payment of all taxes and fees apply to anyone operating a truck in that country. Foreign carriers and drivers also must follow Customs, immigration laws and regulations of the countries in which they are driving.

NAFTA's purposes are specific

The North American Free Trade Agreement, as we said earlier, is a trade agreement between the United States, Canada, and Mexico, establishing free-trade guidelines between the three countries.

When NAFTA was officially signed in November 1993, the agreement itself was fairly simple. What became difficult was the ability for the countries involved to agree on how this agreement would be carried out. Even today, arrangements and agreements are still being negotiated so that NAFTA can be fully initiated.

NAFTA's goals are simply stated. This simplicity is easily illustrated in the NAFTA preamble and purposes, which reads:

The Government of Canada, the Government of the United Mexican States and the Government of the United States of America, resolved:

TO STRENGTHEN the bonds of friendship and cooperation among the nations;

TO CONTRIBUTE to the harmonious expansion of world trade, providing a catalyst to broader international cooperation;

TO CREATE a larger, more secure market for the goods and services produced in their territories;

TO REDUCE distortions to trade;

TO ESTABLISH clear rules governing their trade that are mutually beneficial;

TO ENSURE a predictable commercial framework for business planning and investment;

TO BUILD on their respective rights and obligations under the General Agreement on Tariffs and Trade and other multilateral and bilateral instruments of cooperation;

TO ENHANCE the global competitiveness for their firms in the world-wide marketplace;

TO FOSTER creativity and innovation, promoting trade of goods/services that are the subject of intellectual property rights;

TO CREATE new jobs in all three countries, improving working conditions and living standards for all citizens;

TO UNDERTAKE each of the new trade opportunities in a manner consistent with environmental protection and conservation;

TO PRESERVE their flexibility to safeguard the public welfare;

TO PROMOTE sustainable development and sustainable market growth;

TO STRENGTHEN the development and enforcement of environmental laws and regulations; and

TO PROTECT, enhance and enforce basic workers' rights.

People who glance through NAFTA's goals understandably ask the question, "Yes, all that is fine, but what has NAFTA done for me?" Now, more than 10 years after NAFTA was signed, economists and historians say NAFTA marks the beginning of a period of economic, political, and social growth in North America.

For some companies, NAFTA has boosted their bottom lines. NAFTA has also made Mexico a player in the global marketplace, doing business with some of the world's top automobile manufacturers. It has also increased the world presence of Mexican companies.

United States exports to Mexico grew from $45.29 billion in 1993 to $113.77 billion in 2001. Mexico exported $42.85 billion worth of goods in 1993, a number that exploded to $140.3 billion by 2001.

So, to answer the question, "What has NAFTA done for me?" the jury is still out, but the results appear promising. Suffice it to say, there have been benefits and inroads made so that some products that appear on retailers' shelves make it easier for people of the United States to stretch their dollars further. Sadly, because of the economic downturn, the fear of future terrorist attacks in the United States, the war with Iraq, and the threat from countries that may be developing weapons of mass destruction, the promise of NAFTA has yet to be fully realized.

What is the Land Transportation Standards Subcommittee?

The Land Transportation Standards Subcommittee (LTSS) was established by the North American Free Trade Agreement's (NAFTA) Committee on Standards-Related Measures to examine the land transportation regulatory regimes in the United States, Canada, and Mexico, and to make certain standards more compatible. The Transportation Consultative Group (TCG) was formed by the three countries' departments of transportation. The TCG addresses non-standards-related issues that affect cross-border movements among the countries.

As an example, three LTSS working groups continue to work in trilateral harmonization efforts, including Driver and Vehicle Compliance, Vehicle Weights and Dimensions, and Dangerous Goods/Hazardous Materials. There are also four related Transportation Consultative Groups (TCG) addressing issues not specifically assigned to the LTSS, such as issues relating to cross-border operations and facilitation.

The passage of NAFTA provided a natural continuity for an effort by both the United States and Canada to improve the movement of cargoes and people over the border. With an average flow of more than $1.9 billion worth of goods and more than 300,000 people crossing the border into both countries each day, each government has a huge interest in seeing that their neighboring nations continue to enjoy economic stability.

Because large-scale national events often impact systems and processes across the country, NAFTA's implementation was affected by the terrorist attacks on New York and Washington, D.C. in 2001. After these horrific episodes, Canada's foreign minister and Tom Ridge, Homeland Security Director, co-signed the United States-Canada Smart Border Declaration, outlining a plan to identify and address existing security risks at the border. The plan also attempted to expedite traffic with new processes at the border into each country.

One year later, a status report on the implementation of this effort showed all new processes to be on track. Specifically, it reported that the efforts on both sides of all borders were steadily improving the smooth flow of traffic crossing the border each day.

CHAPTER 2

Crossing into Canada

Cartoon by T. McCracken.

WHAT TO KNOW BEFORE YOU GO

Just as a National Football League (NFL) coach prepares for game day by studying films, designing routes, drawing plays and chalk talks, and putting his playbook together, professional drivers prepare for each trip by studying routing, verifying the roadworthiness of their vehicles, and checking their loads. One of the additional pre-trip preparations required since NAFTA has been for drivers who cross international borders to study and learn the differences in the rules and operating requirements from his or her home base to the point of delivery.

Familiarity with operating requirements, presented here by Canadian provinces, will be a good start in your preparation for a trip into Canada. The charts included are courtesy of the Canadian Government.

Summary of Operating Requirements

Province	Requirements	Single Trip Permits
ALBERTA	• Operating authority in home jurisdiction (buses only) • Cargo insurance/fidelity bond and personal liability/property damage insurance • Alberta corporate registry • United States DOT safety rating • Proof of safety fitness (must be carried in cab)	Maximum of 6 per year
BRITISH COLUMBIA	• Proof of safety fitness • Registered office address in British Columbia • Cargo insurance/fidelity bond and personal liability/property damage insurance	30 day (combined authority and vehicle registration), maximum 2 per power unit per year
MANITOBA	• Proof of safety fitness • Cargo insurance/fidelity bond and personal liability/property damage insurance • Articles of incorporation (or national carrier registration) • Certificate of operating authority from home jurisdiction (Mexico or United States) • United States DOT safety rating	Up to 6 per year
NEW BRUNSWICK	• Must seek specific instructions • Cargo insurance/fidelity bond and personal liability/property damage insurance • Proof of safety fitness, and operating authority from home jurisdiction (Mexico or United States)	Must be purchased before entering New Brunswick

Province	Requirements	Single Trip Permits
NEWFOUNDLAND AND LABRADOR	• Required for buses only • Cargo insurance/fidelity bond and personal liability/property damage insurance • Proof of safety fitness (must be carried in cab)	Not required
NORTHWEST TERRITORIES	Not applicable	Not applicable
NOVA SCOTIA	Required for buses only	Available (buses only)
NUNAVUT	Not applicable	Not applicable
ONTARIO	• Commercial Vehicle Operator's Registration (CVOR) number (or application pending) • Cargo insurance/fidelity bond and personal liability/property damage insurance • Ontario business or agent's address • Bankruptcy statement • Safety fitness test	Available in extenuating circumstances only
PRINCE EDWARD ISLAND	Not required	Not required
QUEBEC	• Copy of Certificate of Incorporation, if a corporation, or national carrier registration • Planned areas of operation in Quebec • Quebec address of head office, domicile or agent with power of attorney • Proof of safety fitness and insurance • Copy of Quebec fuel tax registration certificates • Registration as owner operator (if applicable)	10 day permits available
SASKATCHEWAN	• Safety fitness certificate valid for 5 years • Cargo insurance/fidelity bond and personal liability/property damage insurance • Corporate registration	Available (combined operating authority, vehicle registration, over weight, over dimension, and fuel tax)
YUKON	• Certificate of insurance, endorsed by insurance company • Certificate of incorporation, if a company • For buses, description of proposed routes/schedules • National Safety Code or United States DOT number, or registration in home jurisdiction	Up to 6 per carrier per calendar year

What about insurance?

To resolve the differences between insurance requirements of the three NAFTA countries, a tri-lateral working group comprised of insurance associations, regulators, and transport officials was established to identify insurance issues for cross-border trucking. The NAFTA tri-national Insurance Working Group, operating under the Financial Services Committee, continues to discuss feasible options and find a path toward insurance compatibility. Both short- and long-term objectives and options are being reviewed, with the ultimate objective identified as being mutual recognition, in which one insurance policy is recognized by authorities in all three countries.

In this context, one option considered for cross-border trucking is the Canadian Power of Attorney and Undertaking (PAU) system.

The Canadian PAU system, responding to a need for a common proof-of-insurance coverage for the many United States drivers entering Canada, denotes compliance with minimum insurance coverage requirements. United States insurers may file a PAU with the Canadian Council of Insurance Regulators (CCIR) and then can issue a "yellow card" to United States carriers as valid proof-of-insurance throughout Canada. However, it is common for United States insurers to enter into a "fronting" arrangement with a Canadian insurer, whereby the United States insurer does the underwriting on the United States truck and issues the policy in the Canadian insurer's name, and the Canadian insurer "reinsures" the risk back to the United States insurer.

Recognizing that true mutual insurance recognition would require at least two national governments to change existing insurance regulations, this is more of a long-term objective. A number of more feasible, short-term alternatives under existing laws and insurance regulations are being discussed by the NAFTA Tri-lateral Insurance Working Group:

❏ Brokered Arrangements—Management General Agents (MGAs) are well-established at southern border locations and represent both American and Mexican insurance companies selling coverage to cross-border traffic. The system works fairly well, but requires two separate (back-to-back) policies. MGAs typically arrange advance coverage for carriers for cross-border movement in 12-month intervals.

❏ Joint Ventures—Seen as an outgrowth of brokered arrangements, these are contractual arrangements between insurers to combine coverages and provide seamless insurance (one company "fronts," or issue policies on behalf of the other company).

❏ Fronting Arrangements—An arrangement whereby a domestic insurer takes on the risk of a foreign insurance company and issues a policy on behalf of the foreign insurer. This system is very common, in which

Canadian insurers enter into business arrangements (or joint ventures) with United States companies that front coverage to southbound Canadian carriers. The United States company issues an insurance certificate for the Canadian carrier but doesn't necessarily want to underwrite the risk, so ''re-insures,'' or transfers the risk back to the Canadian insurer.

❑ Canadian Power of Attorney and Undertaking (PAU)—This system, or a system similar to it, as described earlier, is being considered for broader application, encompassing the United States-Mexico border.

What is the CVSA and why do I need to know?

The rules and guidelines of the Commercial Vehicle Safety Alliance (CVSA) are used on all roads across Canada just like they are across the United States and in Mexico. CVSA guidelines are used by inspectors performing roadside inspections of commercial vehicles. If you, your paperwork, or your vehicle do not conform to CVSA guidelines—in Canada, Mexico, or the United States—you risk being placed "out of service" or given a "restricted service condition." Both entail hassle, bringing paperwork and/or vehicle into compliance, fines and/or jail time, depending on the severity of your infraction(s).

Like the United States and Mexico, in Canada you can be put out of service if you are not of legal age to drive, if you do not have a proper license to drive, if you do not pass physical requirements, if you are sick, fatigued or otherwise impaired, or if you are obviously driving under the influence of drugs or alcohol.

You can also be put out of service if you have exceeded the legal number of hours of service, have an incomplete or no driving log, or if your vehicle does not pass inspection.

Unacceptable mechanical problems can include defective brakes, defective coupling devices, defective or missing safety devices, defective exhaust system, defective or missing lighting devices, unsafe loading standards, defective steering mechanisms, defective or inadequate suspension, defective frame, defective or inappropriate tires, wheels and rims, insufficient welds, glazing of the windshield, or defective windshield wipers.

If your vehicle passes a roadside inspection, a CVSA sticker—good for three months—will be placed on your vehicle.

What do I need to know about the International Fuel Tax Agreement (IFTA)?

The IFTA is an agreement among jurisdictions in Canada and the United States for the uniform collection and distribution of fuel use tax revenues. It simplifies the administration, reporting, and compliance by inter-jurisdictional carriers with respect to fuel tax requirements. As most jurisdictions in Canada and the United States collect taxes on gasoline and diesel fuel, the IFTA insures that motor carriers pay their share of fuel taxes. Under the IFTA, motor carriers register in the jurisdiction in which they have an established place of business and the annual fuel taxes owed are apportioned among the IFTA-member jurisdictions in which the carriers travel. Motor carriers deal with a single jurisdiction for fuel tax licensing and reporting.

Fuel Tax

Province	Requirements	Single Trip Permits	Rate Per Litre (cents)
ALBERTA	• Quarterly reports for Alberta-based carriers • Refund for overpayment	Limited to 6	9.0
BRITISH COLUMBIA	• Monthly reports • Credit or refund for overpayment	Up to 6 per vehicle per 6 months	11.5
MANITOBA	• Quarterly reports • Refund of overpayment must be requested within the year	Available	10.9
NEW BRUNSWICK	• Quarterly reports • Refund of overpayment must be requested within 3 years	Available	13.7
NEWFOUNDLAND AND LABRADOR	• Monthly reports	Not issued	16.5
NORTHWEST TERRITORIES	• Monthly reports or deposit • Refund for overpayment	Available	8.5
NOVA SCOTIA	• Monthly reports • Credit for overpayment must be used within the year	Available	15.4
ONTARIO	• Quarterly reports • Automatic refunds for overpayment over $10, less, credit	2–3 days (200–600 km) single trip, only for fleets that travel less than 10,000 km (6215 miles) per year in Ontario	14.3
PRINCE EDWARD ISLAND	• Quarterly reports • Credit for overpayment must be used within the year • No refunds	Available	12.5

Province	Requirements	Single Trip Permits	Rate Per Litre (cents)
QUEBEC	• Temporary permits available under IFTA	3-day single trip, provided fleet makes no more than 5 trips and does not exceed 10,000 km (6215 miles) per year in the province	13.3
SASKATCHEWAN	• Quarterly reports • Credit for overpayment up to $100	As under operating requirements, no refund for any fuel tax paid	15.0
YUKON	• Monthly reports • $300 bond • Refunds for overpayment	At $0.04 per km for single trips	7.2

Note: Mexico is not currently a member of IFTA; the **requirements** listed above may not apply to Mexican drivers in the same way as they would for Canadian and United States drivers.

The International Fuel Tax Association, Inc., is the operational entity for the IFTA. Its web site is www.iftah.org.

IFTA Phone Number for Provinces or Territories

Province	Phone Number
Alberta	(780) 427-3044
British Columbia	(250) 387-0635
Manitoba	(204) 945-5603
New Brunswick	(506) 453-2408
Newfoundland and Labrador	(709) 729-6297
Northwest Territories	(867) 873-7296
Nova Scotia	(902) 424-2850
Nunavut	(867) 645-5165
Ontario	(905) 433-6389 or (905) 433-6412
Prince Edward Island	(902) 368-4070
Quebec	(418) 659-4692
Saskatchewan	(306) 787-7749
Yukon	(403) 667-5345

What is the International Registration Plan (IRP)?

Under the provisions of the IRP, a motor carrier registers in a single jurisdiction (base state or province) and can operate on an inter-jurisdictional basis in other IRP member jurisdictions. The carrier must declare all member jurisdictions in which it will operate, which will be displayed on the cab card, plus the actual or estimated mileage of such operations in each jurisdiction. The registration fees paid by the carrier are divided, or "apportioned," among the IRP jurisdictions in which the carrier will operate, based on a mileage calculation. A carrier's "fleet vehicle" is known as an apportionable vehicle and, so far as registration is concerned, may be operated both inter-jurisdictionally and intra-jurisdictionally. Fifty United States states and all Canadian provinces, excluding the three Territories, are part of the IRP.

The International Registration Plan, Inc., is the operational entity for the IRP.

For further information about IRP, please visit the Website of the International Registration Plan, Inc., at www.aamva.org/IRP/index.asp, or refer to Chapter 3.

IRP Phone Number for Provinces or Territories

Province	Phone Number
Alberta	(403) 340-5430
British Columbia	(604) 443-4450
Manitoba	(204) 945-8915
New Brunswick	(506) 453-2215
Newfoundland and Labrador	(709) 729-3678
Northwest Territories	Not a member of IRP
Nova Scotia	(902) 424-7700 or (902) 424-5536
Nunavut	Not a member of IRP
Ontario	(905) 704-2500
Prince Edward Island	(902) 368-5202
Quebec	(418) 528-4518 or (418) 528-4522
Saskatchewan	(306) 751-1251
Yukon	Not a member of IRP

What if the driver has a criminal record?

All drivers crossing into Canada should be aware that some misdemeanor crimes in the United States are considered criminal offenses in Canada. Canada's immigration laws do not permit entry for drivers with criminal records or a past history of a summary conviction. If you need more information about visiting Canada, go to the Web site at www.cic.gc.ca. Contact the Canadian Consulate so they can classify your conviction. You may require Temporary Entry papers, called a Minister's Permit, which allows one trip. It costs $200, and requires several weeks of processing time. A Discretionary Entry is also a one-time permit allowing you to drive in Canada for up to 30 days. It does not guarantee entry and the fee is $200. A Criminal Rehabilitation, obtained through the Canadian Consulate in the United States, is granted by the Minister of Immigration or the Governor in Council and requires a processing fee of $200. Plan ahead because if you need a special permit to enter Canada, obtaining such a permit usually takes time and money.

What documentation is required?

Any international driver hauling freight into Canada will need the following items and documentation:

1. Your valid commercial driver's license (CDL).
2. Proof-of-citizenship birth certificate, passport, proof of Canadian landed immigrant status (form IMM 1000).
3. Vehicle license and permits, including valid International Fuel Tax (IFTA) and International Registration Plan (IRP) permits.
4. Operating license (also called an operating authority or safety certificate) recognized by each jurisdiction in which you will be traveling.
5. Required number of copies of paper work for Canadian Customs.
6. Some drivers—foreign citizens who are United States residents—may need a visa to be admitted into Canada.

What do I need to know about vehicle registration?

Vehicle Registration

Province	Period	Requirements	Single Trip Permits
ALBERTA	April 1 to March 31	• Proof of ownership • Vehicle import form (if applicable) • Valid insurance • Safety fitness certificate (National Safety Code number) • Identification of registering party • Alberta address and corporate registry (IRP)	Available
BRITISH COLUMBIA	January 1 to December 31	• Valid insurance and license • Safety fitness certificate (National Safety Code number) • Identification of registering party	Single trip or quarterly
MANITOBA	March 1 to February 28/29	• Proof of public liability and property damage insurance (including cargo insurance if a for-hire carrier) • New vehicles must submit the original New Vehicle Information Statement form provided by the manufacturer • Identification of registering party	Available
NEW BRUNSWICK	One Year	• Proof of ownership • Proof of a valid driver's license • Proof of fuel tax registration (IFTA) • Identification of registering party	Available
NEWFOUNDLAND AND LABRADOR	One Year	• Proof of ownership and insurance • Certificate of mechanical fitness for vehicles more than one model year old • Trucks/trailers pay full fees, but charter bus fees are waived if they have a valid registration in their home jurisdiction • Identification of registering party	Available (for truck/trailers)
NORTHWEST TERRITORIES	3 months to one year	• Proof of ownership, financial responsibility and insurance • Not part of IRP • Identification of registering party	Not issued; full registration required
NOVA SCOTIA	One Year	• Proof of ownership and insurance • Registration papers from home jurisdiction (Mexico or United States) • Identification of registering party	30 day

Province	Period	Requirements	Single Trip Permits
NUNAVUT	3 months to one year	• Proof of ownership, financial responsibility and insurance • Not part of IRP • Identification of registering party	Not issued; full registration required
ONTARIO	Staggered 3–15 months	• Proof of registration in home jurisdiction • Proof of empty weight • Canada Customs K22 form (for vehicles imported from the United States) • Proof of ownership • Must register under IRP • Identification of registering party	10 day
PRINCE EDWARD ISLAND	Annual; staggered by birth month of registered owner	• Proof of ownership • Payment of sales tax (IRP) • Fuel tax registration • Identification of registering party	5 day
QUEBEC	April 1 to March 31	• Operating authority (for bulk carriers only) • Proof of ownership • Canada Customs K22 form (for vehicles imported from the United States) • Identification of registering party	10 day
SASKATCHEWAN	One Year Staggered	• Tractor; proof of adequate insurance including $200,000 third party liability • Semitrailer; no further registration required if in possession of valid plates from home jurisdiction • Identification of registering party	As under operating authority
YUKON	One year staggered according to carrier's name	• Certificate of insurance coverage must specify that it is valid for all of Canada, including the Northwest Territories and Yukon • Identification of registering party	Available

What other documents are needed to cross into Canada?

If your trip will involve travel to several provinces, several states or several countries, you are also required to have an International Fuel Tax Agreement sticker (IFTA).

The required registration for the area in which you plan to travel must also be available if you are asked for this documentation. This assures your International Registration Plan (IRP) card is current for all areas in which you will be traveling and will prevent you from paying additional registration fees.

What do I need to know about vehicle weights and heights allowed in Canada?

Under the umbrella of a national agreement (Memorandum of Understanding or MOU), all Canadian provinces have agreed to accept vehicles that comply with a set of national weight and dimension standards for travel on a system of provincial highways designated by each province. In some cases these limits are lower than provincial standards, and in these cases provinces have generally retained the higher limits in regulation.

The provincial and territorial governments also have authority for issuing special permits for oversize and/or overweight loads, movement of selected commodities and other permit provisions that depart from normally regulated limits.

As each province and territory sets and enforces the weight and dimension standards that apply within its boundaries, carriers are advised to consult each province/territory with any questions on acceptable weight and dimension limits, especially with respect to special vehicle configurations.

For specific information, contact the appropriate source listed below:

Contacts for Detailed Information on Vehicle Weight and Dimension Standards

ALBERTA	Director, Transport Engineering Alberta Transportation 4920-51 Street, Room 401 Red Deer, Alberta T4N 6K8 Phone: (403) 340-5189 Fax: (403) 340-5092 E-mail: alvin.moroz@gov.ab.ca
BRITISH COLUMBIA	Manager, Commercial Transport, ICBC Compliance Programs & Standards P.O. Box 3750 Victoria, British Columbia V8W 3Y5 Phone: (250) 414-7900 Fax: (250) 978-8018 E-mail: doug.elliot@icbc.com

(continued)

MANITOBA	Director, Compliance and Regulatory Services Manitoba Transportation and Government Services 1550 Dublin Avenue Winnipeg, Manitoba R3E 0L4 Phone: (204) 945-3898 Fax: (204) 948-2078 E-mail: gcatteeuw@gov.mb.ca
NEW BRUNSWICK	Transportation Policy New Brunswick Department of Transportation P.O. Box 6000 440 Kings St., Kings Place, 2nd Fl. Fredericton, NB E3B 5H1 Phone: (506) 453-2802 Fax: (506) 453-3701 E-mail: denis.goguen@gnb.ca
NEWFOUNDLAND AND LABRADOR	Motor Vehicle Registration Branch Department of Government Services & Lands P.O. Box 8710 149 Smallwood Dr., Mount Pearl St. John's, NF A1B 4J5 Phone: (709) 729-3454 Fax: (709) 729-6955 Email: griffinw@mail.gov.nf.ca
NORTHWEST TERRITORIES	Director/Registrar Road Licencing and Safety Division Department of Transportation P.O. Box 1320 Yellowknife, NWT X1A 2L9 Phone: (867) 873-7406 Fax: (867) 873-0120 E-mail: Gary_Walsh@gov.nt.ca
NOVA SCOTIA	Manager Transportation Policy Development Transportation & Public Works P.O. Box 186 Halifax, NS B3J 2N2 Phone: (902) 424-2490 Fax: (902) 424-1163 E-mail: stonehdo@gov.ns.ca
NUNAVUT	Director of Motor Vehicles Department of Community Government & Transportation Government of Nunavut P.O. Box 207 Gjoa Haven, NU X0B 1J0 Phone: (867) 360-4614 Fax: (867) 360-4619 E-mail: dbuchan@gov.nu.ca

(continued)

ONTARIO	Manager, Vehicle Standards Office Compliance Branch Ministry of Transportation 301 St. Paul Street, 3rd Floor St. Catharines, Ontario L2R 7R4 Phone: (905) 704-2566 Fax: (905) 704-2750 E-mail: ron.covello@mto.gov.on.ca
PRINCE EDWARD ISLAND	Safety Coordinator, Highway Safety Operations Department of Transportation & Public Works P.O. Box 2000, 33 Riverside Dr. Charlottetown, PE C1A 7K8 Phone: (902) 368-5222 Fax: (902) 368-5236 E-mail: wjmacdonald@gov.pe.ca
QUEBEC	Interim chief, Director of Road Transportation of Merchandise Ministry of Transportation 700, boul. René-Lévesque Est, 22e étage Québec (Québec) G1R 5H1 Phone: (418) 644-5593 Fax: (418) 528-5670 Email: gcorbin@mtq.gouv.qc.ca
SASKATCHEWAN	Senior Policy Advisor Trucking Policy & Regulations Unit Saskatchewan Highways and Transportation 1855 Victoria Avenue Regina, Saskatchewan S4P 3V5 Phone: (306) 787-4851 Fax: (306) 787-3963 E-mail: ggilks@highways.gov.sk.ca
YUKON	Manager, Commercial Vehicle Enforcement Yukon Dept of Infrastructure P.O. Box 2703 Whitehorse, Yukon Y1A 2C6 Phone: (867) 667-5920 Fax: (867) 393-6408 E-mail: john.warkentin@gov.yk.ca

WHAT TO KNOW ABOUT CROSSING THE BORDER

In general, to save waiting time and to maintain your projected schedule, you should know the hours of operations of the border crossing you wish to use as well as the hours of operation for the destination where you want to clear Customs.

Non-resident drivers crossing into Canada will need to know when Canadian border crossings are open. For specific information about a particular crossing, call 800-461-9999 or visit the Web site at www.ccra-adrc.gc.ca/customs/general/times/menu-e.html

The following provincial border crossings are open 24 hours a day, 365 days a year. All other border crossings provide service from 8:00 A.M. to 5:00 P.M., Monday through Friday.

Alberta	Coutts Crossing
British Columbia	Pacific Highway, Osoyoos and Kingsgate
Manitoba	Emerson
New Brunswick	Woodstock, St. Stephen
Ontario	Pigeon River, Ft. Francis, Sault Ste. Marie, Sarnia, Prescott, Lansdowne, Ft. Erie, Niagara Falls, Windsor
Quebec	Lacolle, St. Armand-Phillipsburg, Stanhope, Rock Island
Saskatchewan	North Portal

Wait times are usually less than five minutes at most crossings, Mondays through Thursdays. On weekends, wait times may be as much as 20 minutes. Periodically, wait times at the Port Huron, MI bridge can be as long as 45 minutes.

What do I need to know about clearing Customs?

Ancient wisdom tells us, "the more we hurry, the more behind we become." So, the first advice about getting through Customs at any border is to take your time. Relax . . . and smile . . . and always be ready for an inspection. This means have your trailer loaded in such a way that it can be inspected easily. To accomplish this, let the shipper know that the shipment needs to be packed so you will not be delayed at the border.

If you do have waiting time, practice patience—and always be cordial and helpful with inspectors. Also remember, it is a serious offense—under the Customs Act—to leave the border and/or to not report to the compound when requested.

Second, know what your cargo contains so you can answer any questions the Customs inspector may have.

Third, declare all of your personal goods—all of them—and this includes prescription drugs, firearms, or pets. Be prepared to pay duty and taxes, depending on your personal declaration of goods.

If you have contraband in your cab, such as switchblades, butterfly knives or mace, they will be seized and shipped back to your home address—at your expense.

An inspection of your cargo does not carry a cost—and if an inspection fee is charged, report this immediately.

One other point to remember: If you attempt to deliver cargo that has not been released by Customs, your truck and cargo may be seized and you will be additionally punished with a sizable fine.

What should I expect from Customs?

When you first arrive at the border, make certain you are in the appropriate lane and have documentation ready. Also be ready to answer questions from the Customs inspector about your ability to drive in Canada, including your CDL, proof of citizenship, or other paperwork.

Before you begin your trip, make sure that all your shipments are correctly described and documented with the correct form. Also make sure your vehicle is well maintained and can pass a safety inspection at the border, if one is conducted.

Before you get to the border, separate Canadian import forms from United States Customs export forms. This will make the next stops at United States and Canadian Customs much easier.

It is the driver's responsibility to complete the A8A(B) Cargo Control Document. This should be completed before stopping for Customs inspection at the border.

What improvements have been made in Customs paperwork since NAFTA?

As a driver, you don't need an in-depth knowledge of the Customs paperwork required for shipments coming in or out of Canada, but you do need a cursory familiarity so that you can work quickly and efficiently with Customs inspectors at the border. The following information is provided for that purpose:

1. If you, your shipper, or your receiver have questions about the Customs process, the **Small Business Customs Library (SBCL)** is an Internet site developed by the Canadian Customs and Revenue Agency that provides an electronic Customs service 7 days a week, 24 hours a day. The Web site is www.ccra-adrc.gc.ca

   The SBCL site contains general information on importing and exporting, including tariff treatments, duty rates, an exchange rate converter, Customs notices, and news releases. You can also access connections to other Internet sites such as other government departments, foreign Customs administrations, transportation and freight-forwarder sites.

Using the Web site, you may be able to complete and print Form B3, and submit it to your local Customs office. You can also print such forms as Form A and Form B2, *Canada Customs-Adjustment Request,* and complete them by hand.

2. The **In-transit Highway Simplification Project (IHSP)** is a joint effort by the United States Bureau of Customs and Border Protection and Canada's Customs and Revenue Agency. The purpose of the agencies is to expedite documentation requirements for the movement of cargo across Canadian and United States highways. After piloting the system, it was implemented nationally along the United States-Canadian border after both countries signed the joint statement in May, 1999.

   The IHSP process requires two stops: (1) when the carrier provides documentation at the Customs office of the transiting country and (2) at the Customs office of the original country of export.

   The new process cuts down on waiting in the export lanes and offers savings in time (about 30 minutes per trip) and money for carriers.

3. The **Free and Secure Trade (FAST)** program, a joint Canada-United States program, includes the Canada Customs and Revenue Agency, Citizenship and Immigration Canada, the United States Bureau of Customs and Border Protection and the United States Immigration and Naturalization Service. The FAST Program was developed to facilitate the movement of pre-approved eligible goods across the border quickly and to verify trade compliance away from the border.

   Beginning December 2002, Canada and the United States jointly offer expedited Customs clearance processes to pre-authorized drivers, carriers and importers at the following border crossings: (1) Detroit, Michigan / Windsor, Ontario; (2) Buffalo, New York / Fort Erie, Ontario; (3) Lewiston, New York / Queenston, Ontario; (4) Port Huron, Michigan / Sarnia, Ontario; (5) Champlain, New York / Lacolle, Quebec; and (6) Blaine, Washington / Pacific Highway, British Columbia.

   Who is eligible for the FAST Program? Participants include importers, customs brokers, freight forwarders carriers and drivers who have a history of compliance with all relevant rules and regulations, have acceptable record-keeping processes, and well-defined audit trails.

   Shipments for approved companies, transported by approved carriers using registered drivers, will be cleared into either country with greater speed and at reduced cost.

   The benefits of FAST are numerous. They include reduced data requirements for Customs clearance, eliminating the need for importers to send data for each transaction, dedicating FAST clearance lanes, reducing the number of border examinations of cargoes, reducing the need for verifying trade compliance away from the border, and by streamlining accounting/payment processes.

For more information about FAST into Canada, visit the Web site at www.ccra-adrc.gc.ca/customs/business/importing/fast/menu-e.html.

The following are documentation terms drivers may hear or want to know more about as they go through the Customs process at the border:

1. The **Release Notification System (RNS):** Includes four features—automatic release notification, arrival certification, status query, and automatic status. Those authorized to use the automatic release notification feature of RNS can have data confirming release of your goods electronically transmitted in the United Nations Electronic Data Interchange for Administration, Commerce and Transportation (UNEDIFACT). The RNS message can be used to update systems to schedule deliveries or initiate the preparation of accounting data, as well as to electronically notify other parties affected by the release and ensure more timely delivery of your shipments.

2. **Electronic Data Interchange (EDI) Release:** Allows electronic transmission of cargo release data, including invoice information, to the Accelerated Commercial Release Operations Support System (ACROSS). A Customs officer reviews the information and transmits the release decision via the RNS/CADEX Release Notification Report. For more information on EDI release, contact the Electronic Commerce Unit in Ottawa at 1-888-957-7224.

3. The **Customs Internet Gateway:** Initiated in July 2000, this gateway provides an alternative method of transmitting Customs data. Users can transmit their CADEX B3 accounting data, send arrival messages and receive their RNS release messages over the Internet. For more information, contact the Electronic Commerce Unit at 1-888-957-7224 or visit the Web site at www.ccra-adrc.gc.ca/eservices/customs/business/menu-e.html

4. **Foreign Affairs/Customs Automated Permit System (EXCAPS):** Under EXCAPS, importers/ brokers apply for a permit with the Department of Foreign Affairs and International Trade (DFAIT). DFAIT then electronically transmits the permit information. The importer/broker transmits the release information and ACROSS matches the release data to the EXCAPS permit. A Customs inspector then processes the release and permit information, and once the goods are released, a notice is returned to DFAIT informing them that the permit has been used.

5. **Customs Automated Data Exchange (CADEX) system:** An alternative to presenting paper copies of Form B3, *Canada Customs Coding Form*. Customs processes 96% of all the B3 forms received using the CADEX system. This system also provides shippers with access to reports and files to assist in the electronic preparation of Form B3. An authorization to use CADEX, allows the shipper to electronically transmit Form B3 information directly to Canada's Customs computer system over telecommunications lines. For more information on EDI, CADEX, CUSDEC (Customs Declaration), or RNS, contact (613) 954-6341.

6. **Customs/Canadian Food Inspection Agency (CFIA) interface:** Shipments containing commodities that have requirements from this agency may be released by EDI in some locations. The interface serves as a model for the development of similar arrangements with other government departments. To find out how to participate in this interface or to contact this agency in Ottawa, call (613) 952-2996.

7. **Commercial Cash Entry Processing System (CCEPS):** A self-serve automated system designed to facilitate the document preparation process required for the clearance of commercial importations. Personal computers are located at counters in designated Customs offices. Based on importation information that the shipper inputs for goods, CCEPS calculates the applicable duties and taxes. It then generates a completed Form B3.

   A Customs officer enters the data from Form B3 into the ACROSS and forwards the form to the cashier. Once you have accounted for the goods, you will receive a copy of the form stamped "duty paid" and you can take delivery of your goods. In the future, you may be able to complete your own Customs transactions over the Internet, pay duties electronically, and obtain release of imported goods from your own office.

8. **Release on Minimum Documentation (RMD):** By using RMD, a receiver can fast track the release of goods by accounting for and paying for shipments after releasing them. To take advantage of this privilege, post an approved amount of security up to a maximum of $10 million. The goal of this system is to process release requests that are complete, accurate, and do not require examination of goods or review of permits, within the following times: 45 minutes for electronic data exchange, 2 hours for paper documentation.

   Unless the Customs officer opts to examine a shipment, Customs will release it under RMD when the shipper reports the shipment by presenting a completed cargo control document, any import permits or health certificates, and, in most cases, two copies of a properly completed invoice. For more information, call 800-461-9999 within Canada, or 204-983-3500 outside Canada.

9. **AMPS:** The Administrative Monetary Penalty System (AMPS) is a civil penalty regime that secures compliance with Customs legislation through monetary penalties. AMPS largely replaces the use of seizure and forfeiture provisions for technical infractions. Seizure and ascertained forfeiture will only be used for the most serious offences. AMPS imposes monetary penalties in proportion to the type, frequency, and severity of the infraction. Most penalties are graduated and will take the compliance history of the client into consideration. The program does not pose any new obligations to comply with Customs legislation, regulations and undertakings, and will not affect businesses that continue to comply with Customs requirements.

WHAT TO KNOW ABOUT YOUR LOAD

What about in-bond shipments?

If you are hauling an in-bond shipment, when you reach the border, give the Customs inspector a copy of the A8A(B) manifest and follow the instructions from the inspector. Usually, you will be able to move the in-bond shipment to a sufferance warehouse for clearance.

Once you reach the inland warehouse, park in the designated space, which is secured. Then report to the warehouse.

All Customs seals must be intact between the border and the sufferance warehouse clearing the shipment. Do not allow the trailer to be opened until you reach the inland point of clearance. This will save expensive penalties.

Give the Customs broker all required forms for completion and submit the required Customs release documents. Then ask for further instructions or call your dispatcher.

If the inspector at the sufferance warehouse wants to inspect your load visually, it is now permissible to open the trailer for examination. Then the inspector will notify the warehouse operator that the goods have been released and are ready to deliver.

What if I am carrying a mixed shipment?

You may have some cargo that can be released by an inland sufferance warehouse or some that is being hauled for a post audit carrier and some that must pass Customs at the border.

For the items you are taking inland, give the Customs personnel a copy of the A8A manifest and wait for instructions. The Customs broker will complete and submit the required release documents for the shipments requiring clearance. Then, Customs will notify the warehouse of the shipment's status and will, in turn, notify the carrier that the goods have been released and may be delivered.

Once the Customs inspector clears the rest of your load, you can deliver the cargo that has been cleared at the border and then report to the inland sufferance warehouse.

If you are carrying goods for a post-audit carrier, you can proceed to the break-bulk warehouse before reporting to the sufferance warehouse.

What is line release and what are the line release procedures?

Line release is a process that allows shipments to be processed prior to your truck's arrival at the border by the Customs broker or importer and are provided to Customs officials, either electronically or on paper. There are four line release options:

1. **Pre-Arrival Review System (PARS):** Paperwork is sent electronically or faxed to the Customs broker before shipment arrives at the border. The request is submitted to Customs for review and, from there, Customs officials decide whether to inspect the shipment when it reaches the border.

2. **Frequent Importer Release System (FIRST):** Explained in the next section.

3. **Advance Shipment Notification (ASN):** Freight cleared in advance and expedited under ASN, such as automotive shipments, will provide the driver with an A49 form. This form must be completed before your arrival at the border. The Customs inspector will then advise you that your cargo has been released, authorized for delivery, or if further examination is required.

4. **Customs Self-Assessment (CSA):** For approved CSA carriers and importers, this option makes passing Customs simpler and less time consuming. Sponsored by CCRA and Canadian Citizenship and Immigration. For additional information, visit their web site at www.ccra-adrc.gc.ca.

More details about the line release options, PARS, and FIRST

1. **PARS:** This document contains the shipment's estimated time and date of arrival, the invoice data and the original copy of any required permits. PARS documentation/data can be submitted 30 days prior to the shipment's arrival in Canada.

The documentation is processed; the cargo control number is entered into the system with either a recommendation for release or examination. The release recommendation will be ready when your goods arrive if you submit your PARS request at least one hour in advance electronically or two hours in advance on paper. When the truck arrives at the border, it will be released in minutes unless examination is required.

2. **Frequent Importer Release System (FIRST):** Still another line release option to facilitate the speedy release of goods at the border is called Frequent Importer Release System (FIRST). The option is available for importers who have an established record of compliance and receive low-risk, low-revenue goods on a regular basis. With an authorization number identifying FIRST shipments appearing on the importer's pre-approved import document, goods arriving at the border can either be released or referred for inspection, at the discretion of the inspector.

Note: While line release options are designed to simplify border crossings, Customs personnel still have the option of inspecting your cargo.

WHAT TO KNOW WHILE YOU ARE IN CANADA

How do I report an emergency in Canada?

Information is courtesy of the Canadian Wireless Association—more information on wireless 9-1-1 can be found at this web site www.cwta.ca/safety/E911

❑ More than six million emergency calls are made to 9-1-1 each year, using wireless phones.

❑ Approximately 50 percent of all 9-1-1 calls originate from wireless phones.

❑ To report an emergency, dial 9-1-1, give your complete number (mobile phone) and area code.

❑ Also tell the operator your exact location as precisely as possible. Look for street signs, highway markers, and other landmarks.

❑ Stay on the phone as long as you are needed for information. Don't hang up until the emergency operator tells you to do so.

❑ Keep your mobile phone "on" in case the operator needs to call you back.

What do I need to know about Canadian speed limits?

The speed limits in Canada are posted in kilometers per hour as opposed to miles per hour. The speed limit on most city streets is 50 km/hr (30 mi/hr). On most highways, the speed limit is posted as 100 km/hr (60 mi/hr). Speed limits may vary among the provinces, so keep an eye on the posted speed limit signs. A rule of thumb is to multiply the posted speed limit by 6 and then divide by 10 to convert the posted kilometers-per-hour to miles-per-hour.

What do I need to know about money and the Canadian monetary system?

Rates of exchange vary from establishment to establishment. As there are no laws enforcing the rate of exchange on foreign currency, it is wise to change your money at a bank or a reputable currency exchange. Banks are generally open 10:00 A.M. to 4:00 P.M. Monday to Friday. An increasing number are open evenings and Saturday mornings.

Since the exchange rate fluctuates, check with the bank of your choice once you cross the border. To give an example, the exchange rate on August 1, 2003 was one U.S. dollar to 1.39 Canadian dollars; and on November 10, 2003 it was one U.S. dollar to 1.31 Canadian dollars.

Can I bring the dog or cat that rides with me into Canada?

You can bring pet dogs or cats that are three months old or older into Canada from the United States if you have a certificate from a licensed veterinarian identifying the animal by breed, age, sex, coloring, and any distinguishing marks. The certificate must also show the animal has been vaccinated against rabies during the last three years. Animal tags are not acceptable and cannot be used as a substitute for this certificate.

What about bringing firearms into Canada?

Canada has strict laws about firearms. If you plan to bring one into the country, you must declare all firearms at Customs when you enter. If you do not, Customs officials have the right to seize your firearms and you will face criminal charges. For more information regarding a specific firearm or any applicable fees call the Canadian Firearms Center at 1-800-731-4000.

To contact the chief firearms officer of the provinces through which you may travel, call 1-800-731-4000 or contact the Customs office nearest you.

What about the use of alcohol or drugs?

In the United States the Federal Motor Carrier Safety Administration specifically addresses the use of alcohol and illegal drugs for commercial drivers. In Canada, many of the same rules apply. No open containers of beer, wine, or other alcoholic beverages are allowed in your truck. You cannot carry alcohol or illegal drugs in your cab or drive while under the influence of alcohol or illegal drugs.

Canadian officials have the right to test you if they suspect you are driving under the influence of alcohol or illegal drugs. If you test positively, you will be fined and subject to criminal conviction as well as seizure of your vehicle and its cargo.

How long can I drive before rest is required?

Commercial drivers in Canada are allowed to drive 13 hours. Maximum time on duty—and this includes driving time—stands at 15 hours. This requires at least eight hours off duty before you can return to driving or duty. In any seven-day period in Canada, drivers may be on duty for only 60 hours. During an eight-day period, drivers can be on duty a maximum of 70 hours.

What driving records do I have to keep current?

As in the United States, all commercial drivers in Canada are required to maintain up-to-date logbooks. If a driver fails to keep his log up to date, he or she can lose their license to drive, be fined, taken out of service, or be subject to a combination of these penalties. Like the United States, it is against the law to maintain more than one daily log or to falsify the daily log.

If you want to use electronic or other mechanical devices to maintain your daily log, this is permissible as long as the device records all required information and you have signed copies of each log generated for the current trip.

Required information includes (1) the number of hours spent driving each day, (2) the on-duty hours each day, (3) the total on-duty hours accumulated for the current periods of seven, eight or 14 days, and (4) the changes of your duty status and when these changes occurred each day.

Some suggestions for international trucker security

Wherever you are, making an extra effort to assure your personal security and the security of your vehicle and your cargo is always recommended. Here are a few suggestions for safe trips—in any country, at any time:

1. Never leave your vehicle unlocked, even when your engine is idling.

2. Do not leave valuables unattended. Lock them in the motel or truck stop safe.

3. If you spend the night at a motel, make certain the door to your room is locked at all times. For added security, use the night chain or other secondary locking devices.

4. Report all suspicious persons and activities in hallways or parking areas to management.

5. Keep all valuables in your vehicle, out of sight.

6. Do not carry large amounts of cash. Use traveler's cheques and credit cards as much as possible. If needed, carry cash in a money belt under your clothing.

7. While out walking, remain in well-lighted and well-traveled areas. Do not take short cuts through darkened areas.

Some facts about Canada

❑ There are 31,485,623 people living in Canada. About 10 times this number live in the United States.

❑ Quebec has the highest annual snowfall with 337 cm.

❑ Highest point in Canada is Mt. Logan in the Yukon at 5,959 meters.

❑ In Canada, the infant death rate is lower and the life expectancy is longer than in the United States.

❑ Every product in Canada is labeled in English and French.

❑ Canadians use the metric system to measure everything. (See Appendix M for conversion of metric units to United States measurements.)

❑ Canada contains almost 10 million square kilometers of land, 891,163 square kilometers of water.

❑ Good News! Canada has more donut shops per capita than the United States.

❑ Sports fans in Canada favor hockey (surprise!) and lacrosse.

❑ St. John's Nova Scotia is the wettest area of Canada, receiving 1,482 millimeters of rain each year.

❑ Canadian stamps must be used when mail is sent from Canada. Rates are 47 cents within Canada, 60 cents to the United States, and $1.05 to countries overseas.

❑ There are $1 and $2 coins—and prices appear to be higher than in the United States because of the Canadian monetary system. For exchange rates, visit www.bankofcanada.ca.

❏ The Trans-Canada Highway is usually two-lanes wide. The 401 highway north of Toronto is 16 lanes wide in places.

National holidays: **January 1**—New Year's Day[1]; **April 9**—Good Friday[2]; **April 12**—Easter Monday[2]; **The Monday on or preceding May 24**—Victoria Day; **July 1**—Canada Day[1]; **First Monday in September**—Labor Day; **Second Monday in October**—Thanksgiving Day; **November 11**—Remembrance Day[3]; **December 25**—Christmas Day[1]; **December 26**—Boxing Day[1].

Helpful references for truckers

For truckers planning to drive extensively in Canada, there are two documents available—one titled "Crossing International Borders—A Trucker's Guide" and "Road Signs and Rules: A Trucker's Guide." These may be ordered from the Ontario Trucking Association. Please call (416) 249-4071, or send an email to info@ontruck.org, and ask for a product catalogue.

---

[1]When these days fall on a Sunday, the next working day is considered a holiday. If Canada Day falls on a Saturday or Sunday, the Monday following is a holiday.

[2]The dates shown here are for the year 2004. As these dates are moveable holidays, check Canadian calendars for information on current years.

[3]Officially Government offices and banks only, though in practice many other businesses may close.

CHAPTER 3

Crossing into Mexico

"Hmm…November 2nd. It must be the Day of the Dead."

Cartoon by T. McCracken.

INTRODUCTION

When a professional commercial driver drives in Mexico, he or she should remember that import/export laws and customs are changing in Mexico because of the changing political climate of all of North America, security concerns, and changing NAFTA rules.

Due to these changes, many cross-border consultants are now available to work with United States and Canadian carriers wanting to do business in Mexico. There are also Customs brokers, who must be hired to assist in smoothing the road between one country and another.

WHAT TO KNOW BEFORE YOU GO

What kind of driver's license will I need?

The United States Commercial Driver's License is valid in Mexico. Mexican insurance is required for all vehicles, including rental vehicles.

What about hours of service for drivers in Mexico?

Since hours of service and vehicle inspections are safety issues and your employer probably has high expectations regarding hours of service and vehicle inspections, the driver should not neglect them regardless of the laws of the host country.

During what hours do the border crossings and Customs offices operate?

The hours of operation for United States and Mexican Customs offices vary from site to site. Generally the hours of operation of Mexican Customs offices coincide with the United States Custom offices in the same area. Most United States Custom offices are open 24 hours a day, 365 days per year. The driver should be aware that some Mexican custom offices may be closed during Mexican holidays The hours of operation at a driver's intended crossing can be supplied by the Mexican Customs agent hired to assist with the border crossing.

What about alcohol or drugs?

Although the laws about alcohol and drug use may not be as strict in Mexico as in the United States, drivers in Mexico should follow the same guidelines as they follow in the United States or Canada. As a professional, the driver does not do anything that would contribute to an unsafe act; therefore, there should be no use of drugs and/or alcohol. The driver should be reminded again that they are in a foreign country and that their load and vehicle can be confiscated if there is an accident or violation of Mexico's laws.

May I take my child with me when I drive in Mexico?

In an effort to prevent international child abduction, many governments have initiated procedures at entry and exit points, including requiring documentary evidence of relationship and permission of the parent(s) or legal guardian not present for the child's travel. Parents of minor children (under 18 years old) should document carefully legal custody prior to traveling anywhere. If a minor child is traveling with only one parent, the absent parent should provide notarized consent. If only one parent has legal custody, that parent should be prepared to provide such evidence to Mexican authorities. In cases in which a minor child is traveling alone or in someone else's company, both parents (or the sole, documented custodial parent) should provide notarized consent. If a child has a different last name from the mother and/or father, the parents should be prepared to provide evidence to airlines and Mexican authorities, such as a birth certificate or adoption decree, to prove that they are indeed the parents.

What should I know about communications?

Of the population over age 15 in Mexico, almost 90 percent can read. The principal language of the country is Spanish. English is also spoken, particularly in larger communities.

WHAT TO KNOW ABOUT CROSSING THE BORDER

What paperwork will I need?

The Mexican Government's requirements for paperwork are one of those areas that continue to evolve.

At this writing, Canadian truckers are allowed to cross the border into Mexico and to transport freight to and from Mexican terminals under the agreement called the "Memorandum of Understanding" (MOU), signed in 1994. A driver entering the country under the MOU should have a valid driver's license, a clean criminal record, proof of Canadian citizenship, and paperwork authorizing him or her to work as a professional driver for a specific company.

The government of Mexico requires that all United States citizens present proof of citizenship and photo identification for entry into Mexico.

A United States passport is recommended, but other United States citizenship documents such as a certified copy of a United States birth certificate, a Naturalization Certificate, a Consular Report of Birth Abroad, or a Certificate of Citizenship are acceptable. Driver's permits, voter registration cards, affidavits, and similar documents are not sufficient to prove citizenship for re-admission into the United States.

When crossing the border into Mexico, operators of freight services must declare any amount of money in cash or checks when these exceed $10,000. Drivers are also required to declare any merchandise that may be related to contraband activities, in accordance with Article 105 of the Federal Tax Code.

What if I have dual citizenships?

As of March 20, 1998, Mexican law recognizes dual nationality for Mexicans by birth, meaning those born in Mexico or born abroad to Mexican parents. United States citizens who are also Mexican nationals are considered to be Mexican by local authorities. Therefore, their dual-nationality status could hamper United States Government efforts to provide consular protection. Dual nationals are not subject to compulsory military service in Mexico. Travelers possessing both United States and Mexican nationalities must carry with them proof of their citizenship of both countries. Under Mexican law, dual nationals entering or departing Mexico must identify themselves as Mexican.

What are the FMN and the FMN3?

Drivers who fall under the definition of "business visitors" may use the FMN or FMN3 forms for entry into Mexican territory. These forms may be obtained from Mexican Consulate offices in Canada and the United States.

To obtain an FMN form, provide migratory officers with an original document confirming nationality, including signature and photograph. This may also be a passport or certified copy of a birth certificate. Also required is a letter on company stationery outlining the activities to be conducted in Mexico.

The Non-immigrant Business Visitor's Form, FMN3, is used when the driver will be in Mexico for more than 30 days. Required documentation is the same as for an FMN. If the driver holds an FMN and applies for an FMN3, the FMN should be handed to the application officer for cancellation.

If the FMN or FMN3 form expires before the driver leaves the country, the fine should be paid before leaving the country.

What if I lose my identification in Mexico?

If you lose your United States passport or other identification, report this immediately to the nearest United States embassy or consulate. United States citizens may refer to the Department of State's pamphlet, *A Safe Trip Abroad*, for ways to promote a trouble-free journey at www.access.gpo.gov or via the Bureau of Consular Affairs' home page at www.travel.state.gov.

For further information concerning entry and visa requirements, travelers may contact the Embassy of Mexico at 1911 Pennsylvania Avenue N.W., Washington, D.C. 20006, telephone (202) 736-1000, or its Web site at www.embassyofmexico.org or any Mexican consulate in the United States.

What if I become ill while driving in Mexico?

Foreign drivers should be aware that excellent health facilities are available in Mexico City. Care in more remote areas is limited. Americans may consult the United States Embassy's Web site or the United States Embassy, a consulate or consular agency (see addresses in Appendix H) prior to seeking medical attention. The Embassy's Web address is www.usembassy-mexico.gov.

Doctors and hospitals often expect immediate cash payment for health services, and United States medical insurance is not always accepted. You may wish to have the attending doctor explain procedures and costs before undertaking treatment. The Department of State strongly urges Americans to consult with their medical insurance company prior to traveling abroad. Useful information on medical emergencies abroad, including overseas insurance programs, is provided in the Department of State's Bureau of Consular Affairs brochure, Medical Information for Americans Traveling Abroad, available via the Bureau of Consular Affairs home page or fax: (202) 647-3000.

More information for drivers working in Mexico

In many areas in Mexico, tap water is unsafe and should be avoided. Bottled water and beverages are safe, although visitors should be aware that many restaurants and hotels serve tap water unless bottled water is specifically requested. Ice may also come from tap water and should be considered unsafe. Visitors should exercise caution when buying food or beverages from street vendors. Mild abdominal cramps and diarrhea are to be expected when traveling to a new environment. Fever, chills, and bloody diarrhea suggest infection from contaminated food or water, and should be aggressively treated with fluid and electrolyte replacement (Gatorade, Pedialyte, etc.).

In high-altitude areas such as Mexico City (elevation 7,600 feet or about 1/2 mile higher than Denver, Colorado), most people need a short adjustment period. Reaction signs to high altitude include a lack of energy, shortness of breath, occasional dizziness, headache, and insomnia. Those with heart problems should consult their doctor before traveling. Air pollution in Mexico City and Guadalajara is severe, especially from December to May and when combined with high altitude, could affect travelers with underlying respiratory problems.

WHAT TO KNOW ABOUT YOUR LOAD

According to information published by the Office of Texas State Controller Carole K. Strayhorn, the following guidelines were being used, effective February 1, 2003:

Crossing southbound from the United States

Commercial vehicles entering Mexico are subject to two levels of inspection comprising a series of stops before the vehicle is cleared to proceed to its destination in the Mexican border zone or beyond. The first inspection is conducted by the Mexican Customs broker in the United States and the second inspection by the Mexican Customs Service in Mexico.

Pre-border crossing activities in the United States

Prior to arrival at the carrier's facility in the Texas border zone, a United States Customs broker arranges with a Mexican Customs broker for payment of duties and delivery of import documents to Mexican Customs. The cargo remains in the border zone until the payment for duties has cleared Mexican banks. Duties must be paid prior to arriving at the border crossing. Toll collection is done by the United States owner-operator of the bridge. Generally, tolls are collected manually or through computer-accessed corporate accounts.

Bridge crossing

The international crossings between the United States and Mexican Customs facilities also carry mixed traffic non-commercial and commercial vehicles. All non-commercial and commercial vehicles from the United States proceed through a primary inspection point located on the Mexican side of the bridge.

Mexican crossing activities

Only loaded trucks and vehicles being imported into Mexico are subjected to the Mexican truck inspection process. Empty trucks and tractors without trailers pass through inspection with all the passenger vehicles. A central computer recognizes the document bar code and selects the trucks for primary inspection.

Mexican primary inspection

The primary inspection is a freight-only inspection. All trucks undergo the same inspection. Commercial vehicles completing the primary inspection may be selected to undergo a secondary inspection.

Secondary inspection in Mexico

Some of the trucks completing the primary inspection are selected for the secondary inspection. The secondary inspection repeats the primary inspection, but it is conducted by a private contractor.

Mexican exit inspection

Documents are reviewed to ensure that the necessary inspections are conducted before the commercial vehicle is allowed to proceed to its final destination in Mexico.

The documents needed to enter Mexico with a commercial tractor-trailer must be filled out in Spanish or they may be in English if accompanied by a Spanish translation. Having as many documents completed as possible before arrival at the border will greatly reduce the time needed for crossing. This could reduce the time needed to cross the border from hours to minutes.

A Mexican Customs broker must be hired. The broker will fill out all forms and permits and will accompany the driver through the process of clearing Mexican customs.

There are two ways to clear the shipment at the border. These are (1) move the shipment in-bond to another inland site for clearance or (2) clear the shipment at the border.

Declaring the shipment in-bond

Shipping freight in-bond into Mexico is very similar to Canada and the United States with the following exceptions: (1) the bond is not posted by the carrier but by the importer or exporter and (2) the carrier must be registered with Mexican Customs.

On arrival at the border and after clearing United States Customs, the driver proceeds to Mexican Customs where the Mexican Customs broker is met. The Mexican Customs broker will prepare the required documents and submit them to the Mexican Customs inspector. After the documents are prepared and submitted, the driver will be instructed to drive to the inspection station. At this time the driver will be instructed to proceed to the intended destination or to the inspection area. The driver should carefully follow the instructions of the Mexican Customs broker and the Mexican Customs inspectors.

What does a Customs broker actually do?

Customs brokers work with importers, exporters, shippers, and freight forwarders to get the necessary information to prepare documents required by United States and Mexican Customs laws and regulations. Documentation duties are similar for United States and Mexican Customs brokers for exports to Mexico. Mexican Customs brokers appraise the shipment, classify the goods according to the tariff schedule, and inspect and inventory the cargo.

Mexican law requires United States shippers to use Mexican Customs brokers at the border—doing business on the United States side.

Where do I find a Mexican Customs broker?

According to sources at the Market Access and Compliance Section of the United States Department of Commerce, the Mexican importer of United States products generally hires a broker. However, the best way to find a broker is through recommendation. If you are unable to find a broker, you may contact the Confederacion de Asociaciones de Agentes Aduanales de la Republica Mexicana at 011-525-533-0075, 011-525-533-0076, 011-525-533-0077, or 011-525-533-0683.

How can I clear my shipment at the border?

The driver will proceed to Mexican Customs, where the freight will be processed by the Mexican Customs inspectors. If all the documents are filled out correctly and the rig is not the one in ten that is chosen for inspection, the driver may proceed to his or her destination.

What is a Certificate of Origin?

There are two types of Certificates of Origin that Mexico may need—the NAFTA certificate of origin or the certificate of origin to determine the country of origin for non-NAFTA goods.

A Word about forms needed to cross the border

Due to the changing political climate in all of North America, security concerns and changes in NAFTA and in tariff laws, the information and forms needed to cross the border will evolve for many years to come. Therefore, a driver should not attempt to cross the border without help from a Mexican Customs broker. Information about Mexican Customs forms and brokers are found at the end of this book.

WHAT TO KNOW WHILE YOU ARE IN MEXICO

What should I know about Mexico's telephone system?

Domestic: Offers 12 main lines per 100 persons. Adequate service is available for business and government. The use of cellular telephones is common for much of the domestic service. International: Numerous satellite earth stations are giving Mexico improved access to South America, Central America, and much of the United States. Check with your communications provider to determine the availability of cellular telephone service in Mexico.

How do I get assistance in an emergency?

If you have an emergency while driving, the equivalent of "911" in Mexico is "060," but this number is not always answered. If you are driving on a toll highway or "cuota," or any other major highway, you may contact the "Green Angels," a fleet of trucks with bilingual crews that operate daily. The "Green Angels" may be reached directly at (01) 55 5250-8221. If you are unable to call them, pull off the road and lift the hood of your truck. Chances are they will find you.

What do I need to know about buying diesel fuel in Mexico?

Gasoline prices in Mexico are government-controlled. Prices fluctuate with the economy. There is only one grade of diesel fuel in Mexico and it is sold in liter measures. One liter is close to one quart. Four liters equal about one gallon. To convert liters to gallons, divide the number of liters purchased by four to calculate how many gallons you have purchased.

Look for the black sign signaling that diesel fuel is being sold at that location.

What if I have legal problems while in Mexico?

While in Mexico, United States and Canadian citizens are subject to Mexico's laws and regulations, which sometimes differ significantly from those in the United States and may not afford the protections available to the individual under United States law. Visitors who commit illegal acts have no special privileges and are subject to full prosecution under the Mexican judicial system. Penalties for breaking the law can be more severe than in the United States or Canada for similar offenses. Persons violating Mexico's laws, even unknowingly, may be expelled, arrested, or imprisoned.

What are the penalties for drug offenses?

Penalties for drug offenses are strict and convicted offenders can expect large fines and jail sentences of up to 25 years. As in the United States, the purchase of controlled medications requires a doctor's prescription. The Mexican list of controlled medications differs from that of the United States, and Mexican public health laws concerning controlled medications are unclear and often enforced selectively.

Further information on bringing prescription drugs into the United States is available from the United States Customs Service at www.customs.ustreas.gov.

Also, the United States Embassy cautions that possession of any amount of prescription medicine brought from the United States, including medications to treat HIV and psychotropic drugs, such as Valium, can result in arrest if Mexican authorities suspect abuse or if the quantity of the prescription medicine exceeds the amount required for several days' use. Individuals should consider carrying a copy of the prescription and a doctor's letter explaining that the quantity of medication is appropriate for their personal medical use. United States citizens who may be in possession of medication prescribed in the United States should check with the nearest Mexican consulate before traveling to Mexico.

What are the penalties for firearms violations?

The Department of State warns United States citizens against taking any type of firearm or ammunition into Mexico without prior written authorization from the Mexican authorities. Entering Mexico with a firearm, some kinds of knives, or even a single round of ammunition is illegal, even if the firearm or ammunition is taken into Mexico unintentionally. Firearms and ammunition of a caliber higher than .22 are considered to be for the exclusive use of the military, and their importation carries penalties of up to 30 years in prison. The Mexican government strictly enforces its laws restricting the entry of firearms and ammunition along all land borders and at airports and seaports. Violations have resulted in arrests, convictions, and long prison sentences for United States citizens.

At the time of this writing, a rancher from Texas is in a prison in Mexico for taking a box of ammunition into Mexico. Being raised on the border, he knew he could not take a firearm into Mexico. He left his pistol, which he usually carried in his truck, at home, but forgot about a box of ammunition under the seat. He was unlucky enough to be driving the one out of ten vehicles that is inspected by Customs and is now in prison. His defense was that he forgot and it was only a box of shells. "Forgot" and "only" is not a good defense in Mexico.

The only way to import firearms and/or ammunition into Mexico legally is to secure a permit in advance from the Mexican Embassy in Washington, D.C., or from a Mexican consulate, even if the firearm is legally registered in the United States.

What are the penalties for smuggling aliens?

Mexican authorities may prosecute anyone arrested for transporting aliens into or out of Mexico for alien smuggling in addition to any charges they may face in the other country involved, including the United States. Alien smuggling and harboring aliens is a serious felony offense in Mexico. If the incident involves a child, prison sentences of five years are routine.

What should I know about driving in Mexico?

A Primary Rule: Never do anything unexpected but always expect the unexpected.

Mexico has an extensive highway system. This system consists of privately owned limited-access toll roads, state-owned limited-access toll roads, national divided highways, national two-lane highways, secondary paved roads, and many miles of dirt roads.

Just as in Canada and the United States, the limited-access toll roads have the widest lanes, the widest shoulders and the least amount of traffic. The private toll roads compared to the state toll roads typically have wider lanes and shoulders and less traffic. Most drivers report that the privately owned toll roads are in better repair than the state toll roads.

The private toll roads are usually more expensive than the state-owned toll roads but the expense is often offset by less traffic, smoother and better-repaired roads, less of a grade in mountainous regions, and a more direct route to one's destination.

The best choice—if toll roads are not available—are the national divided highway system. These roads are not maintained as well as the toll roads. The lanes may be narrower and the shoulders will be narrow or nonexistent compared to toll roads, and the volume of traffic will be much greater on these roads. Most of these roads will loop around small cities and villages but may go through larger cities. If the road does go through a city, a driver can expect the traffic to be extremely heavy.

Avoid two-lane highways! The lanes are extremely narrow, the shoulders will be very narrow or they may be nonexistent and they are usually choked with cars, buses, and trucks of all sizes. Fortunately, most of the roads from the United States border to the major manufacturing and trade centers in Mexico are toll roads or divided highways.

Are traffic signal lights different in Mexico? All professional drivers should be especially cautious when approaching intersections controlled by stop signs or traffic signals—in any country. Compared to signals in the United States and Canada they may be very dim. Also there is no set pattern for their location. They may be in the middle of the intersection or on a pole (maybe a short pole) near the intersection. Be extremely cautious at these intersections. Some cities have traffic signals that flash green several times before the amber comes on. Many drivers consider this a signal to speed up in an effort to get through the intersection before the red signal comes on.

What about detour signs? In Canada and the United States, usually detour signs are numerous and conspicuous along a detour route and may even have instructions pertaining to the detour. In Mexico, detour signs are smaller and after the first one there may not be another for miles. Look carefully for the detour signs and just keep on going. After many blocks in a city or miles in a rural area another sign will appear.

How do I handle one-lane bridges? On many of the older rural roads and in some small cities bridges are one-lane. When two vehicles approach a one-lane bridge from different directions the first to blink their lights has the right of way.

What are the methods of warning of obstructions ahead? When driving on rural roads, if someone waves a piece of cloth at you, or you encounter a series of beer bottles placed on the road, or a series of rocks placed on the road, you can be sure that a stalled vehicle is just around the next curve or over the next hill.

Speed bumps or tope (TOE-pay in Spanish). Speed bumps are quite severe in many rural areas. If one does not drive over them at walking speed, there could be extensive damage to a rig and its cargo.

Do not drive at night except on toll roads. Accident statistics show that more than 80 percent of the fatal traffic accidents in Mexico happen at night. There are many reasons for this. Just as in Canada and the United States, alcohol consumption goes up at night. Some parts of Mexico are extremely poor and many vehicles do not have taillights. Much of rural Mexico is not fenced and cattle or horses may be on the road. As many rural roads do not have much of a shoulder, pedestrians generally walk on the road.

Some facts about Mexico

Information provided by The World Fact Book 2002—an Internet of the Central Intelligence Agency—www.odci.gov/cia/publications/factbook/geos/mx.html.

❑ **Official Name:** The United Mexican States (*Estados Unidos Mexicanos* in Spanish).

❑ **Geography:** Covers approximately 761,600 sq. miles.

❑ **Population:** 103,400,165 (July 2002 estimation).

❑ **Capital City:** Mexico City (*Distrito Federal* in Spanish).

❑ **Number of States:** Thirty-one and one Federal District. Each state is headed by an elected governor.

❑ **Major Transportation Centers:** Border cities—with connections to major interior cities—Tijuana to Baja California; Nogales to the Pacific Coast; Ciudad Juarez to Chihuahua, Torreon, Monterrey, San Luis Potosi, Mexico City, and Guadalajara; Nuevo Laredo to Monterrey, San Luis Potosi, Mexico City and Guadalajara; Reynosa and Matamoros to Monterrey, San Luis Potosi, Mexico City, and Guadalajara.

Interior cities—Chihuahua, Monterrey, San Luis Potosi, Guadalajara, Mexico City.

❑ **Miles of highways (paved):** Total 60,000 miles, of which 4,000 miles are expressways (estimated 1997).

❑ **Climate:** Varies from tropical to desert with high rugged mountains, low coastal plains, and high plateaus. Mexico's climate is generally more closely related to altitude and rainfall than to latitude.

❑ **Economy:** An estimated 40 percent of all Mexican citizens live below the poverty line. Main crops are corn, wheat, soybeans, rice beans, cotton, fruit, coffee, tomatoes, beef, poultry, dairy products, and wood products.

❑ **Industries:** Food and beverages, tobacco, chemical, iron and steel, petroleum, mining, textiles, clothing, motor vehicles, consumer durables.

❑ **Export commodities:** Manufactured goods, oil and oil products, silver, fruits, vegetables, coffee, cotton.

❑ **Export partners:** United States 88.4 percent, Canada 2 percent.

❑ **Import partners:** United States 68.4 percent, Canada 2.5 percent.

❑ **National holidays**

Mexico has a number of government recognized national holidays when banks, post offices, government offices, and many shops and businesses are closed:

January 1—*Año Nuevo*—New Year's Day.

February 5—*Día de la Constitución*—Constitution Day—Commemorates Mexico's Constitution.

February 24—*Día de la Bandera*—Flag Day—Holiday to honor the Mexican flag.

March 21—*Día de Nacimiento de Benito Juárez*—Birthday of Benito Juárez, a famous Mexican president and national hero.

May 1—*Día del Trabajo*—Labor Day—equivalent to the United States Labor Day.

May 5—*Cinco de Mayo*—The celebration of Mexico's victory over the French army at Puebla de los Angeles in 1862.

May 10—*Día de la Madre*—Mother's Day—Due to the importance of the mother in Mexican culture, Mother's Day is an especially significant holiday.

September 16—*Día de la Independencia*—Independence Day, commemorating the beginning of Mexico's war of independence from Spain.

October 12—*Día de la Raza*—Means literally "day of the race," commemorating Columbus's discovery of the New World and the founding of the Mexican (mextizo) people.

November 1—*Informe Presidencial*—the President's state of the nation address to the legislature, coinciding with the Catholic *Día de Todos Santos* (All Saints' Day).

November 20—*Día de la Revolucion*—Revolution Day—Anniversary of the Mexican Revolution of 1910.

December 25—*Día de Navidad*—Christmas Day.

❑ **Other national celebrations**

Though not official holidays, some of the following are among the most important festivals in the Mexican calendar:

January 6—*Día de los Reyes Magos*—Three Kings' Day—The day when Mexicans exchange Christmas presents in accordance with the arrival of the three gift-bearing wise men to Jesus Christ. This day culminates the Christmastime festivities.

February 2—*Día de la Candelaría*—Candlelight processions and dancing in many towns.

Late February or Early March—*Carnaval*—Carnival—A holiday that kicks off a five-day celebration of the libido before the Catholic lent. Beginning the weekend before Lent, Carnaval is celebrated exuberantly with parades, floats, and dancing in the streets. Similar to Mardi Gras in the United States

March or April—*Semana Santa*—Holy Week—This week before Easter is one of Mexico's biggest holiday periods, beginning on Palm Sunday and ending on Easter. It officially ends the 40-day Lent period. It is the Mexican custom to break confetti-filled eggs over the heads of friends and family. Millions of Mexicans take the family on a "holiday" during this period.

November 1 & 2—*Día de los Muertos*—Day of the Dead—The celebration for when dead relatives, both young and old, are allowed to return to the mortal world for two days to visit loved ones. Spirits come down, walk among the living, sample earthly treats, and join in the festival. The people in Mexico welcome the spirits of their families with the delicious smell of food in the air, tasty candies decorated like skulls, and lighted candles to guide them home again. Gravestones are decorated, and the whole family will gather in the graveyard to await the arrival of the spirits and to pay respects to those who have already passed on.

December 12—*Día de Nuestra Señora de Guadalupe*—Day of Our Lady of Guadalupe—Celebrated with a feast honoring Mexico's patron saint.

December 16–24—*Las Posadas*—Posadas are literally "inns," but in this case they refer to Joseph and Mary's search for shelter in Bethlehem and feature candlelight processions that end at various nativity scenes. *Las Posadas* continues through January 6.

CHAPTER 4

Crossing into the United States

U.S. BORDER

"When I ask you to present a photo I. D., I didn't mean pictures of your wife, kids, dogs and mother-in-law."

Cartoon by T. McCracken.

INTRODUCTION

With the passage of the North American Free Trade Agreement (NAFTA), plans called for motor freight companies from Canada, the United States, and Mexico to move freely across North America. NAFTA's visionaries believed that open borders would not only encourage movement of international cargo but also promotion of foreign investment.

To date, NAFTA permits Mexican trucking firms to provide cross-border delivery and the backhaul of cargo. Canadian trucking companies operate in the United States under an agreement that was made prior to NAFTA. Neither Mexican nor Canadian trucking companies are authorized to move domestic cargo from point to point in the United States, a reciprocal agreement for all three NAFTA countries.

All foreign motor carriers operating in the United States are subject to the same federal and state regulations that apply to United States carriers, including safety regulations, insurance requirements, and labor and environmental standards. Foreign carriers must also pay the same taxes and fees. In addition, foreign motor carriers and drivers must comply with appropriate customs and immigration laws.

Today, a truck crosses the border into the United States from Canada every 2.5 seconds. Year-to-date truck-transported goods to the United States from Canada, as of May 2003, had a total worth of $21,562,000. Year-to-date for the same period, truck-transported goods from Mexico had a total worth of $13,545,000. The increase in trade between the United States and Mexico, and to a lesser degree between Mexico and Canada, has dramatically increased the demand for trucking services. At this writing, approximately 85% of trade between the United States and Mexico is by truck.

There is still work to be done—particularly in an effort to open the border between the United States and Mexico. More agreements are waiting to be negotiated and more work on harmonization is needed, but the opportunities for international shipping continue to increase among the three NAFTA countries.

WHAT TO KNOW BEFORE YOU GO

What is the Federal Motor Carrier Safety Administration (FMCSA) and why do I need to know about it?

FMCSA works to maintain safety on the highways and in the operation of motor carriers in the United States. This agency regulates all commercial vehicles operating in the United States and publishes the operational guidelines. FMCSA headquarters are located in Washington, DC and it has offices in every state in the United States as well as Service Centers in Atlanta, GA; Baltimore, MD; Olympia Fields, IL; and San Francisco, CA. The FMCA Web site can be found at www.fmcsa.dot.gov. A Spanish-language version is available at www.fmcsa.dot.gov/spanish.

FMCSA operates a toll-free hotline for reporting actual or potential violations of its regulations. This number is 1-888-368-7238 or 1-888-DOT-SAFT. Written comments or complaints may be sent to FMCSA, 400 Seventh Street, SW, Washington, DC 20590 or faxed to 202-366-7298.

What are the operating hours of the border crossings into the United States?

Most of the major border crossings along the Canadian and Mexican borders are open 24 hours a day, 365 days a year. Smaller crossings may have limited hours. It is always wise to check the status of a crossing before you arrive.

What are the laws concerning driver logbooks?

It is important to keep your logbook complete and up-to-date, listing the proper hours of service regulations. Failure to do so could mean that you may be fined, be placed out-of-service, or have your license revoked.

What about a driver's hours of service in the United States? (For a full explanation, see Chapter Five)

Effective June 27, 2003, a driver may drive up to 11 hours in any 14-consecutive-hour on-duty period. No driver may drive after having been on duty for 14 consecutive hours. The rule allows a driver to perform non-driving work after having been on-duty for 14 consecutive hours.

A new exemption allows a short haul driver to drive after the 14th hour, but not after the 16th hour, one day a week. The new rule does not require a rest break during an on-duty shift. No driver may drive after being on duty 60 hours in any 7 consecutive days. For carriers that operate 7 days a week, no driver may drive after being on duty 70 hours in 8 consecutive days.

What do I need to know about immigration requirements?

Foreign drivers may apply for admission to the United States as visitors for business (B-1 classification) and must meet the following general entry requirements: (1) Must have a residence in the country from which they are traveling, (2) must intend to depart the United States at the end of the authorized period of temporary admission, (3) must have adequate financial means to carry out business while in the United States, and (4) must prove that he or she is not inadmissible from the United States for health-related reasons, past criminal record, involvement in subversive activity, improper manner of arrival in the United States, or improper documents.

What about driving conditions in the United States?

Most major roadways are well maintained with periodic rest areas for all highway users. If you will be driving in mountainous areas or areas of extreme temperatures, such as the desert in summer or northern climates during the winter months, be prepared for any emergency situation with appropriate clothing, blankets, bottled water, food staples, communications equipment, and emergency equipment, such as triangles, flares, and fire extinguishers.

WHAT TO KNOW ABOUT CROSSING THE BORDER

What documentation and other items do I need to cross the border?

Canadian citizens entering the United States do not require either a passport or a visa. Generally, an oral declaration may be accepted or the inspecting officer may require documentation, such as a passport, birth certificate, or certificate of citizenship. Due to increased security measures, all visitors may be required to present photo identification.

Mexican citizens entering the United States as business visitors are required to provide: (1) A valid Mexican passport containing a valid B-1/B-2 non-immigrant visa provided by a United States Consulate. Consulates in Mexico also issue a combination B-1/B-2 visa and Mexican Border Crossing Card serving the same purpose. (2) For DSP "Laser Visa," a credit card-like document that serves as a Border Crossing Card and a B-1/B-2 visa. These can be obtained from a United States Consulate in Mexico City, Ciudad Juarez, Guadalajara, Hermosillo, Merida, Matamoros, Monterrey, Nogales, Nuevo Laredo, Tijuana, and Mexicali.

Visa information can be obtained by calling 01-900-849-3737 or by visiting the United States Embassy on the Web.

If entering for more than 72 hours or traveling beyond 25 miles of the Mexican border, drivers will be issued Form I-94, the Arrival-Departure Form, for completion. To expedite this process, motor carriers delivering freight beyond the border state area may complete Form I-94 prior to arrival at the point of entry. Fee for an I-94 form is $6.00 for visitors.

All drivers also need:

- ❏ A valid commercial driver's license (CDL).
- ❏ Vehicle license and permits, including valid International Fuel Tax (IFTA) and International Registration Plan (IRP) permits.
- ❏ Operating license (also called operating authority or safety certificate) recognized by each jurisdiction in which you will travel.
- ❏ Customs paperwork.

What licensures and other documents will I need?

It is important to make sure you have all the proper licenses and registrations for your vehicle and your commercial driver's license is current. For interprovincial, interstate, and international travel, you should have a current International Fuel Tax Agreement (IFTA) sticker.

Your vehicle must have the required registration for the area in which you plan to travel. This means make sure that your International Registration Plan (IRP) card is current for all areas in which you will be traveling. This will ensure that you don't have to pay any further registration fees.

What do I need to know about operating authority?

Federal Authority and a United States Department of Transportation (DOT) number is necessary when operating a commercial motor vehicle in the United States Federal authority can be granted as a Common, Contract, Household Goods, or Passenger Vehicle.

You must file for operating authority if you are crossing an international line or state line for hire. You must have the new FMCSA authority with the United States DOT number (the DOT number signals that FMCSA has granted a carrier operating authority).

An OP1-MX or OP2 application must be filed for Mexican companies to operate beyond the border commercial zones, or within the commercial zones respectively. Only OP2 applications are being processed presently.

What do I need to know about obtaining a Certificate of Registration for Mexico-domiciled motor carriers?

All carriers must have a Certificate of Registration to operate in the United States on the United States/Mexican border or within the commercial zones of these municipalities. Mexico-domiciled carriers who operate at acceptable levels of safety performance and pass the safety audit will be issued a permanent Certificate of Registration at the end of an 18-month provisional period. Once Mexico-domiciled carriers have a permanent Certificate, they will fall under the same safety requirements and operational procedures applied to United States and Canadian carriers. For more information, call the Federal Motor Carrier Safety Administration's Information Line at 001-800-832-5660 from Mexico or 1-800-832-5660 from the United States or Canada.

What do I need to know about immigration requirements for Canadian drivers?

Canadian truck drivers must meet the general entry requirements as a visitor for business. These include (1) having a residence in a foreign country with no intention of abandoning; (2) intent to depart the United States at the end of an authorized period of temporary admission; (3) having adequate financial means to carry out the purpose of the visit and departure from the United States; and (4) establishing that the driver is not inadmissible to the United States under Section 212(a) of the Immigration and Naturalization Act, which includes as grounds for inadmissibility such things as health, criminal subversive, public charge, improper manner of arrival or improper documents, other immigration violations, and other categories.

What is cabotage?

The Federal Motor Carriers Safety Administration has published the following requirements related to cabotage. The word "cabotage" refers to the point-to-point transportation of property or passengers.

Foreign motor carriers are required to comply with United States Customs rules and regulations about cabotage while in the United States. Foreign drivers are required to comply with Immigration rules and regulations relating to entry into the United States and performance of work while in the United States. In most cases, the Immigration and Naturalization Service (INS) and United States Customs regulations are consistent, but a few differences do exist. To be in full compliance, both the foreign driver and the foreign-based vehicle must comply with the appropriate regulations.

Generally, foreign carriers are prohibited from engaging in domestic traffic in the United States. Foreign carriers are allowed to make international moves. Determinations of the type of traffic—domestic or international—are based on the origin and destination of the cargo.

The movement of empty vehicles between two points in the United States is not considered a domestic move. Foreign carriers are allowed to reposition empty vehicles within the United States.

In-transit cargo refers to the transportation of merchandise having both a United States origin and destination that travels through Canada or Mexico.

Generally the use of foreign-based vehicles for domestic movement of merchandise is prohibited. There is one exception—a domestic movement incidental to the immediate, prior, or subsequent engagement of a vehicle in international transportation is allowed. For example, a Toronto-based carrier moves merchandise from Toronto to Miami, FL. The vehicle can then pick up merchandise in Miami for delivery in St. Louis, where an export move will be picked up for delivery to Canada. The merchandise move from Miami to St. Louis is considered incidental to the immediate, prior, or subsequent use of the vehicle in international transportation.

These changes were made in cabotage regulations to allow more efficient and economical use of vehicles, both domestically and internationally.

What should I know about Customs personal exemptions?

If you are a United States citizen returning to the United States, you may qualify for a personal exemption. Personal exemptions allow you to bring goods of a certain value back to the United States without paying duties and taxes.

WHAT TO KNOW ABOUT YOUR LOAD

What does it take to get my cargo through Customs?

Cargo, whether duty is owed on it or not, must clear Customs at the first port of arrival in the United States. If you choose, you may have your freight sent, while it is still in Customs custody, to another port for Customs clearance. This is called *forwarding freight in bond*. You (or someone you appoint to act for you) are responsible for arranging to clear your merchandise through Customs or for having it forwarded to another port.

Frequently, a freight forwarder in a foreign country will take care of these arrangements, including hiring a Customs broker in the United States to clear the merchandise through Customs. Whenever a third party handles the clearing and forwarding of your merchandise, that party charges a fee for its services. This fee is not a Customs charge. When a foreign seller entrusts a shipment to a broker or agent in the United States, that seller usually pays only enough freight to have the shipment delivered to the first port of arrival in the United States. This means that you, the buyer, will have to pay additional inland transportation, or *freight forwarding* charges, plus brokers' fees, insurance, and possibly other charges.

What do I need to do to clear Customs if I'm coming into the United States from Canada or Mexico?

When you arrive at Customs, the inspector will ask you several questions to determine your immigration admissibility. You may need to show proof of citizenship and residency.

If you are importing any goods for personal use, including prescription drugs and firearms, declare them now. Be prepared to pay duty and taxes if required. Failure to declare personal goods could result in seizure of goods and the truck.

The inspector may ask to examine the cab and your shipment. Be cordial and courteous, presenting the forms required by Customs to the United States Customs inspector.

To speed Customs clearance, the import community and the Customs Service have created the *Customs Automated Commercial System (ACS)*, which electronically receives and processes entry documentation and provides cargo disposition information. Cargo carriers, Customs brokers, and importers may use the system, which reduces clearance time from days to hours or even minutes. Persons entering into the importing trade who intend to file their own entry documentation with Customs are encouraged to explore this method of transacting business. Also, those importing merchandise either for their own use or for commercial transactions may use a Customs broker who transacts Customs business using the *Automated Broker Interface (ABI)* in combination with ACS.

What is the Cargo Selectivity System?

The ACS Cargo Selectivity System is used to sort high-risk cargo from low-risk cargo and to determine the type of examination required. The Cargo Selectivity System accepts data transmitted through ABI and compares it against established criteria. ACS or In-bond entries processed through the Cargo Selectivity System are automatically posted to the appropriate bill of lading. Cargo Selectivity facilitates faster cargo processing.

What does "Border Cargo Selectivity" mean?

The Border Cargo Selectivity System was designed to determine risk assessment and examination requirements. The system uses the same editing process as the Cargo Selectivity system. ABI filers can also transmit manifest information through this system.

What is Entry Summary Selectivity?

The ACS Entry Summary Selectivity System automates the review of entry summary data. Using line item data transmitted through ABI, the system matches national and local selectivity criteria against entry summary data to assess risk by importer, tariff number, country of origin, manufacturer, and value. The entry summary selectivity system captures paperless summary activity, discrepant summary findings, and line item team assignment data.

What does it mean to declare a shipment "In-bond?"

For a shipment to be moved inland you must be a bonded carrier. Once you reach Customs, give the inspector the 7512, Transportation Entry and Manifest of Goods Form. If the shipper did not complete the form you can either complete it yourself or have a Customs broker complete it for you. The Customs inspector will stamp "RELEASE" on your copy of the 7512, seal the trailer, and give you an in-bond card and a form 6512C. You will then drive on to your inland point of clearance where you will park your trailer at the designated area.

Provide the completed forms required by Customs to the broker, who will complete and process the necessary forms to obtain release of goods.

What do I need to know about clearing the shipment at the border, coming northbound from Mexico?

At this point in NAFTA's history, the movement of Mexican freight across the border is facilitated by drayage drivers. When governmental bans are lifted, the following, in part, will be the process to follow:

All forms must be presented to the Mexican Customs broker, who processes the forms and then forwards them to the Mexican Customs inspector. The inspector—once the process is complete—will instruct the driver to move to the export inspection station. If the inspector directs you to open your trailer, do so courteously and wait for the inspection. Your cargo may be unloaded for inspection and checked against your paperwork. Do not leave this area until you are directed to do so. Next, report to the United States Customs inspector, who will ask you questions about your ability to cross the border, and will ask for your citizenship papers. Provide all the required forms to the United States Customs inspector, who may also ask to inspect your cab as well as your trailer and your load.

Then, according to the documentation of your load, either follow in-bond or line release procedures.

What is the "Border Release Advanced Screening & Selectivity" (BRASS)?

The BRASS system tracks and releases highly repetitive shipments at land border locations. A Customs inspector scans a bar code into a personal computer, verifies that the bar code matches the invoice data, enters the quantity, and releases the cargo. The cargo release data is transmitted to ACS, which establishes an entry and the requirement for an entry summary, and provides ABI participants with release information.

If line release or bonding is not being used, before proceeding to the United States, unprepared drivers must stop, park their trucks at a staging area, deliver paperwork to a document processing attendant, await affixation of a unique bar code to each commercial invoice and truck manifest, and make sure paperwork is faxed to Customs brokers in the United States. Once the documentation has been submitted to the United States Customs Service, drivers are allowed to proceed.

What is the FAST Program?

The Free and Secure Trade (FAST) program is a joint Canada-United States initiative involving the Canada Customs and Revenue Agency, Citizenship and Immigration Canada, the United States Customs Service, and the United States Immigration Service.

FAST supports moving pre-approved eligible goods across the border quickly and verifying trade compliance away from the border.

It is a harmonized commercial process offered to pre-approved importers and carriers, and registered drivers. Shipments for approved companies, transported by approved carriers using registered drivers, will be cleared into either country with greater speed and certainty, and at reduced cost of compliance.

A carrier or importer interested in becoming FAST approved should consult
www.ccra-adrc.gc.ca/customs/business/importing/fast/menu-e.html

For more information, call 866-340-FAST (3278).

What are the benefits of the FAST program?

FAST, based on sound risk management techniques, focuses on greater speed and certainty at the border and reduces the cost of compliance by:

- ❏ Reducing the information requirements for Customs clearance
- ❏ Eliminating the need for importers to transmit data for each transaction
- ❏ Dedicating lanes for FAST clearances
- ❏ Reducing the rate of border examinations
- ❏ Verifying trade compliance away from the border
- ❏ Streamlining accounting and payment processes for all goods imported by approved importers (Canada only)

How to apply for FAST

Applications for United States bound carriers must be sent to the United States FAST Processing Center, 50 South Main Street, Suite 100R, St. Albans, VT 05478 U.S.A. For more information, email: industry.partnership@Customs.treas.gov.

What is C-TPAT and who qualifies for membership?

In 2002, the Bureau of Customs and Border Protection (formerly the Customs Service) introduced the Customs Trade Partnership Against Terrorism (C-TPAT) program. The basic requirements are simple—companies must have total knowledge of their supply chain vendors using security guidelines developed by the Bureau. They also must ensure their vendors employ these same security measures to safeguard shipments entering the United States and provide Customs with specific and relevant information about their trucks, drivers, cargo, suppliers, and routes.

For additional Customs information, call 1-877-CUSTOMS or visit the United States Customs Service's Web site at www.customs.gov.

WHAT TO KNOW WHILE YOU ARE IN THE UNITED STATES

Be Alert! United States government officials may check your logbook, vehicle maintenance, licenses, and other items related to the safety of your vehicle. Failure to maintain safety regulations will result in costly and lengthy delays.

How do I report an emergency?

Dial 9-1-1 in every part of the country for emergency response. Stay on the line until you have reported your location and the nature of the emergency. If you use a cell phone, hang up only after the 9-1-1 operator has given you the okay. Keep your phone on in case they need to call you back.

What do I need to know about drugs and alcohol in the United States?

As in most countries, it is illegal to have alcohol in your cab, be under the influence of any substance that would impair your driving, or possess any type of illegal drug. A positive test could result in a fine, criminal conviction, and/or the seizure of your vehicle.

In addition the United States has federal substance testing regulations covering both alcohol and drugs. This means you may need to take a drug test in your home state before you leave or following any type of accident you have in the United States. Records at your work place are subject to audit by United States regulations.

What vehicle safety standards should I know about?

The United States Department of Transportation has set up specific safety requirements for motor carriers operating within the United States. For a full listing of the rules, visit www.fmcsa.dot.gov and click on NAFTA.

Certified federal and state safety inspectors will be required to inspect and verify the status and validity of the license of each over-the-road driver in the United States.

What should I know about CVSA inspections and decals?

The Commercial Vehicle Safety Administration issues a decal for vehicles that pass a rigorous CVSA inspection. If a vehicle has a recent CVSA decal, it will probably not be inspected if stopped on the highway for a random inspection.

Most random inspections are Level I North American Standard Inspections—including examination of driver's CDL, medical examiner's certificate and waiver (if applicable), alcohol and drugs, driver's log and hours of service. The vehicle inspection includes seat belts, brake system, coupling devices, exhaust system, frame, fuel system, turn signals, brake lamps, tail lamps, head lamps, lamps on projecting loads, safe loading, steering mechanism, suspension system, tires, van and open-top trailer bodies, wheels and rims, and windshield wipers.

What does the CVSA vehicle inspection include?

The following is the procedure used to inspect commercial motor vehicles. Those passing the inspection will be issued a CVSA decal. Those failing the inspection will be taken out of service and cannot proceed without proper repairs and a successful inspection: (1) interview driver; (2) collect driver's documents; (3) check for presence of hazardous materials; (4) identify carrier; (5) examine driver's license; (6) check medical examiner's certificate and waiver; (7) check record of duty status; (8) review driver's daily vehicle inspection report; (9) review periodic inspection report; (10) prepare driver for vehicle inspection; (11) inspect front of tractor; (12) inspect left front side of tractor; (13) inspect left saddle tank area; (14) inspect trailer front; (15) check left rear tractor area; (16) inspect left side of trailer; (17) inspect left rear trailer wheels; (18) inspect rear of trailer; (19) inspect right rear trailer wheels, rims and tires; (20) inspect right side of trailer; (21) inspect right rear tractor area wheels, rims, and tires; (22) inspect right saddle tank area, right fuel tank(s); (23) inspect right front side of tractor wheels, rims, and tires; (24) inspect double and triple trailers; (25) test low air pressure warning device; (26) check steering wheel lash; (27) test air loss rate; (28) inspect steering axle; (29) inspect axle(s) 2 and/or 3; (30) inspect axle(s) 4 and/or 5; (31) check brake adjustment; (32) inspect tractor protection system—this procedure tests both the tractor protection valve and the emergency brakes; (33) check fifth wheel movement; (34) complete the inspection paperwork; (35) take appropriate enforcement action; and (36) apply CVSA decal.

What is the North American Standard Cargo Inspection?

An inspector will check the following to determine if a load meets the standard: (1) check shipping paper compliance; (2) check placarding compliance; (3) check marking compliance; (4) check labeling compliance; (5) check packaging compliance; (6) check loading compliance; (7) check securement and integrity of equipment; (8) check piping protection; (9) check double bulkhead drains; (10) check valves and closures; and (11) check rear-end protection/rear bumper.

Some facts about the United States

❑ The 2002 estimated population was 280,562,489, of which 65% were between the ages of 16 and 60.

❑ There are 48 contiguous states; Hawaii and Alaska bring the total to 50.

❑ The lowest point is Death Valley, California. The highest point, Mt. McKinley, Alaska.

❑ The United States covers about 9 million square kilometers.

❑ Life expectancy is 77-plus years.

❑ Approximately 97% of all Americans over 16 are literate.

❑ The Protestant faith is the largest religion, followed by Catholicism and Judaism.

❑ English is spoken almost everywhere, with Spanish as a second language gaining momentum across the country.

❑ Postage is 37 cents per letter.

❑ 12% of all Americans live below the poverty line.

❑ Average income is about $34,000.

❑ Federal holidays (affect all Federal government offices and the District of Columbia): January 1—New Year's Day; January 20—Inauguration Day; Third Monday in January—Martin Luther King Jr. Day; Third Monday in February—Presidents' Day/Washington's Birthday; Last Monday in May—Memorial Day; June 14—Flag Day; July 4—Independence Day; First Monday in September—Labor Day; Second Monday in October—Columbus Day; November 11—Veteran's Day; Fourth Thursday in November—Thanksgiving; December 25—Christmas Day.

Holidays occurring on a Saturday are observed on the preceding Friday, those on a Sunday on the following Monday.

Miscellaneous information

Each state within the United States offers a great deal in the way of scenery and historic sites as well as museums, monuments, and other sites of interest. To make the most of your trip—if time allows—find out about each state in which you will travel so you can be on the lookout for natural wonders as well as other interesting sights.

CHAPTER 5

Hours of Service Rules

"I don't keep track of my hours of service anymore.
Ask my OBR."

Cartoon by T. McCracken.

REVISED UNITED STATES HOURS OF SERVICE

Until June 2003, the United States transportation industry had been regulated by the original rules of service developed for the industry in 1939. In 2003, the final format for new hours of service rules was released with a compliance date of January 4, 2004.

Changes in the hours of service rulings for United States drivers were made because of improved roadways, improved equipment, and more comfort for drivers. Increased research into driver alertness and causes of driver fatigue also played a role in the hours of service revision.

The new regulations apply only to cargo carriers. Vehicles carrying passengers will continue operating under the previously existing rules. The new regulations apply as well to Mexican and Canadian drivers and carriers operating in the United States. During periods of driving in the United States, Mexican and Canadian drivers must maintain a current record of duty status for the previous 7/8 consecutive day period.

The new ruling specifies 14 consecutive on-duty hours, with a maximum of 11 driving hours. Drivers can work a cumulative on-duty schedule of 60 hours in 7 days or 70 hours in 8 days (for carriers operating 7 days a week). Required off-duty hours were increased to 10—and each duty period must begin with at least 10 hours off-duty rather than the previously required 8 hours of off-duty time.

If a driver is on-duty but not driving within a 24-hour period, the driver may remain on-duty for more than 14 hours. However, the driver cannot drive after the 14th hour after coming on-duty. The new rule also reduces subsequent on-duty time available under the 60/70-hour rule.

Waiting time is considered on-duty but is not considered driving time.

The new hours of service rules also specify a sleeper berth exception that states drivers may split on-duty time by using sleeper berth periods, but must comply with new hours of service rules. Drivers using sleeper berths may accumulate the equivalent of 10 consecutive hours off-duty by taking two periods of rest in the sleeper berth—if these guidelines are followed:

(1) Neither rest period is less than 2 hours

(2) Driving time in the period immediately before and after each rest period, when added together, does not include any driving after the 14th hour.

Other exceptions:

The new industry exception to hours-of-service specifies that oil field operations, construction and equipment operations, and utility service, vehicle operations must comply with the new 11-hour driving, 10 consecutive hours off-duty and 14 hours on-duty requirements of the new rules. However, the 24-hour restart provisions applicable to these operations remain in effect.

If a carrier allows a driver to log mealtime as off-duty time, this time does not extend the 14-hour on-duty workday. However, time logged as off-duty is not counted in calculating a driver's 60/70-hour on-duty period.

FMCSA is determined that electronic on-board recorders (EOBRs) will not be required. However, FCMSA plans to conduct expanded research into EOBRs and other technologies and may provide incentives for the universal use of electronic on-board recorders or alternatives in the future.

PENALTIES FOR VIOLATING HOURS OF SERVICE RULES

Drivers or carriers violating the new rules after the implementation deadline of January 4, 2004 will face the following serious penalties:

❑ Drivers may be placed out-of-service (shut down) at the roadside until the driver has accumulated enough off-duty time to be back in compliance.

❑ State and local law enforcement officers may assess fines.

❑ FMCSA may levy civil penalties on the driver or carrier, ranging from $550 to $11,000 per violation, depending on the severity.

❑ The carrier's safety rating will be downgraded for recurring violations.

❑ Federal criminal penalties can be brought against carriers who knowingly and willfully allow or require hours-of-service violations.

MEXICO HOURS OF SERVICE

There are no hours of service specified by law in Mexico at this time.

CANADA HOURS OF SERVICE

Existing regulations have changed little over the last 60 years. Much more is now known about the causes of fatigue as well as its prevention and countermeasures. Proposed regulations would bring Canada's Hours of Service regulations in line with the latest scientific thinking.

Proposed regulations will provide a 25 percent daily average increase in off-duty time from 8 to 10 hours, as well as a daily reduction in working time from 16 to 14 hours. New regulations also call for the elimination of the cycle switching provisions of the existing regime that now allow drivers to legally drive up to 104 hours in a week.

Existing regulations lack the flexibility to enable drivers to choose the work/rest rotation best suited to them. This proposal would average on- and off-duty time over a 48-hour period, allowing drivers more flexibility to rest when needed. New regulations incorporate adequate rest and recovery periods at the end of duty cycles, while minimizing the amount of down time drivers must spend away from home.

As the Hours of Service Rules currently stand, a motor carrier shall not request, require, or permit a driver to drive after accumulating 13 hours of driving time following at least 8 consecutive hours off-duty or after accumulating 15 hours on-duty time following at least 8 consecutive hours off-duty.

A motor carrier cannot request, require, or permit a driver to drive after accumulating 60 hours of on-duty time during a period of seven consecutive days; after accumulating 70 hours of on-duty time during a period of 8 consecutive days; or after accumulating 120 hours of on-duty time during a period of 14 consecutive days.

A driver may not accumulate more than 75 hours of on-duty time without taking a minimum of 24 consecutive hours of off-duty time.

Proposed changes awaiting a review by the Commons Transport Committee would allow 14 hours of on-duty time, and would not distinguish between hours worked and hours driven. Current rules allow 13 hours of driving time and a total of 15 hours of so-called "on-duty" time.

CHAPTER 6

HAZMAT—What You Need to Know

"Been haulin' Hazmat 30 years.
How'd ya know?"

Cartoon by T. McCracken.

The mission of the Federal Motor Carrier Safety Administration (FMCSA) is to improve truck and bus safety on United States highways. FMCSA's primary measure of their success in accomplishing this mission is reducing the number of commercial truck-related fatalities. Their goal—by 2010—is to reduce commercial truck-related fatalities by 50 percent and to reduce the number of persons injured in large-truck crashes by 20 percent.

Although deaths and injuries due to exposure to hazardous materials in transportation are not included in the calculation of truck-related fatalities or injuries, FMCSA has an important secondary goal—to reduce the number of serious hazardous materials transportation incidents.

WHAT DO THE RECENT HAZMAT RULINGS REQUIRE?

The United States Transportation Department's Research and Special Programs Administration has designed new security planning and training rules for HazMat transported in the United States.

The new rules require carriers of placarded HazMat loads or shipments regulated by the Centers for Disease Control and Prevention to create and implement special security plans. The rules also ask companies to give all HazMat employees security awareness training and more in-depth training for those people responsible for implementing the security plan.

Deadline for the new plan to be in place was September 25, 2003, with general training completed by March 25, 2006. More in-depth training should be completed no later than December 22, 2006.

Carriers hauling less dangerous HazMat would be required to produce minimal plans. Again, in-depth training is required only for employees involved in implementing HazMat security plans.

WHAT ARE THE DRIVER'S RESPONSIBILITIES WHEN HAULING A HAZMAT LOAD?

In the transport of hazardous materials, drivers have these responsibilities:

1. They should receive specialized training—required by United States federal law—before they can accept shipments of hazardous materials.

2. They also need the hazardous materials endorsement on their Commercial Driver's License.

3. A trained tractor-trailer driver must have the ability—as well as the legal responsibility to:

❑ Check the bill of lading for hazardous materials cargo

❑ Make sure shipping papers are complete and accurate

❑ Check shipping papers to assure the shipper's certification has been signed

❑ Check packages for proper labeling and marking

❑ Check the compatibility and segregation requirements for the hazardous cargo

❑ Observe the special handling and loading requirements

❑ Properly placard the vehicle, as required

❑ Comply with all FMCSA hazardous materials rules

Since some HazMat loads cannot use certain roadways, always check the shipping papers for special routing instructions. If the driver must plan his or her route, avoid restricted roads, bridges, tunnels, or heavily populated areas.

WHAT DOES A DRIVER NEED TO KNOW ABOUT HAZMAT PLACARDS?

Placards are diamond-shaped signs used to identify the hazard class of a HazMat load. Placards must be displayed on each side of the vehicle. Placards are used to communicate that this is a hazardous load and for traffic to stay a safe distance away from the HazMat vehicle on the highway.

Placards are important not only to over-the-road traffic but also to communicate the type of contents in the load to emergency responders if the vehicle carrying HazMat is involved in an emergency situation. Placards must remain on empty tanks and tank trucks until they are cleaned after hauling a HazMat load.

WHAT DOES A DRIVER NEED TO KNOW ABOUT HAZMAT LABELS?

Like placards, labels are used on packages of HazMat to communicate the hazardous nature of the packages' contents. United States Federal law requires materials meeting the definition of more than one hazardous class to display multiple labels.

Before hauling a HazMat load, the professional driver must check to see that packages within the load are properly labeled.

WHAT DOES A DRIVER NEED TO KNOW ABOUT HANDLING HAZMAT SHIPPING PAPERS?

When hauling a mixed load with some HazMat and some cargo that is not HazMat, put the HazMat cargo's shipping papers or bills of lading on top of the stack of shipping papers and place them in a driver's pouch.

This pouch should be kept on the seat within reach of the driver when the seatbelt is fastened—throughout the trip. If the driver leaves the truck, the pouch should be left in the driver's seat or in the door pocket—within easy reach of any emergency responders if an accident occurs.

HAZARDOUS MATERIALS AREAS AND PACKAGING CONTROLS

Until specific security measures are completed and put into practice, the following measures are being used for HazMat loading and delivery areas and should be of interest to drivers responsible for the security of their rigs and their cargoes:

❑ Are facility grounds adequately lighted?
❑ Are HazMat loads located in a secure area?
❑ Are transport vehicles located in a secure area?
❑ Is access to HazMat limited and/or monitored with sign-in, sign-out clearance?
❑ Do employees working in the area wear ID badges or carry ID cards?
❑ Is a guard force appropriate—particularly on Department of Defense loads, poisonous-by-inhalation materials, radioactive materials, DOE shipments and others?
❑ Are security alarms, video surveillance cameras, security guards, or other security measures being used?
❑ Are records required when HazMat is moved from secure locations?
❑ Are employees trained and reminded to be aware of activities in their areas at all times?

❑ Are keys, entry cards, and ID cards regularly tracked and inspected—
and is special attention paid to those keys, entry cards, and ID's issued
to employees who are no longer with the company?

In some instances, shippers are resorting to electronic tagging, such as
electronic chips inserted into each package or each unit to be shipped.
This type of tagging makes it easier to track shipments that may be
stolen, tampered with, or otherwise mishandled. Drivers should
be aware of this type of tracking device if it is included in a shipment.

WHAT ARE THE MAXIMUM FINES IN HAZMAT CASES?

The minimum fine for a HazMat violation is $275. The maximum
civil penalty for violation of federal hazardous materials regulations is
$32,500. The penalty assessment will be at the discretion of the Research
and Special Programs Administration based on a company's violation
history.

CHAPTER 7

Basic Security

"Sometimes Joe takes the security thing a bit too far."

Cartoon by T. McCracken.

Security has always been a major part of a professional driver's job. Every year, millions of dollars in cargo and equipment is stolen, and while much is recovered, much more disappears. This type of theft, pilferage, and loss is costly to consumers, to carriers, and to you, the driver.

Prior to September 11, 2001, and the destruction of the World Trade Center towers, most Americans—indeed, much of the world—thought terrorist activities happened in some other country, certainly not in their own backyards.

It is now obvious that terrorism is a very real danger in this hemisphere and will continue to be a concern for years to come.

Historically, motor vehicles of all kinds, particularly trucks—because of their larger capacities—have been used as means of delivery for terrorist activities. And, there is every reason to believe that terrorist activities using trucks as delivery systems will continue to be real threats to the safety of Americans everywhere.

Think back a few years to the Oklahoma City bombing. The delivery device was a rented straight truck—and the destruction caused by the bomb used was horrendous.

Car bombs are used all over the world today, taking down buildings and destroying lives in their wake.

But, back to trucks as weapons of mass destruction and the possibilities: A B-52 bomber can deliver 2,000 pounds of precision munitions per bomb within 10 meters of its target. A tractor-trailer rig has the capacity to deliver 40,000 pounds of precision munitions within 10 meters of its target.

The use of this illustration is not to strike fear in the hearts of the public and the professional driver population. It is, however, used to build awareness that the terrorist will try to use any means to bomb a target, using any available weapon—including your rig.

It is, therefore, the responsibility of every professional driver to be aware of the possibilities of their rigs being used to perpetrate a terrorist's mission—and it is also the driver's responsibility to prevent the use of their rig and those of their fellow drivers as weapons of mass destruction.

TRUCKING SECURITY GROWS INTO A LARGER ISSUE

Since the events of September 11, 2001, the area of transportation security has gained much additional attention, from every level of government. Now, because the North American continent realizes that terrorists do not just want to topple buildings and kill people but, simply, to cripple entire countries, experts in terrorism have warned that the trucking industry is a ripe target for the next round of terrorist activities.

During an address to the Truckload Carriers Association in 2002, Ken Allard, a retired army officer and security and information intelligence analyst for MSNBC cable network, made this assessment: "The goal of terrorists is not to destroy our buildings and kill our citizens. They want to destroy our economy and our way or life. Terrorism is a threat to everything we do and to everything we stand for."

James Hall, former chairman of the United States National Transportation Safety Board, addressing the same group said this: "The challenge for trucking is to build security into operations in the same way that safety has been promoted. With narrow profit margins and increasing insurance premiums, many executives will question how to pay for increases in security. For instance, federal, state, and local officials have called for new and redundant background checks and identification procedures for transportation employees. If enacted, some of these proposals could bankrupt many trucking companies. Trucking is vulnerable to terrorists. Added expense along with increased paperwork will do little to relieve that vulnerability, so the first step toward defeating terrorists is to understand the nature of the threat."

"Understanding the threat shows that vulnerability is not limited to the security of company facilities, employees, or loads. Attacks on customers or suppliers can harm truck lines just as badly as an attack on the company," he continued. "An attack on infrastructure, such as power supplies or water sources, could severely damage a local economy," he said, adding that no one could afford to adopt security measures that do not work or that ruin the transportation economy in the process.

Hall did encourage carriers and professional drivers to:

❑ Make plans for alternate communication systems in case of primary telephone or radio network damage.

❑ Testing these plans will ensure the back-up systems are working at all times.

❑ Use the company safety program to build security awareness throughout the entire company, not just among drivers.

❑ Identify key emergency management officials in areas in which the carrier operates. Contact these officials and set a procedure for getting in touch with them at any time.

❑ Drivers and their satellite tracking and communications systems can become the eyes and ears of America.

INCREASING YOUR RIG'S SECURITY

One of the lessons learned from September 11th is this: Never underestimate the enemy or the potential danger of any situation. If something doesn't seem right, call the police, the FBI, or your company/dispatcher—immediately.

Security on the road

❑ Be alert when leaving a location. Criminal surveillance often begins at, or near, your origin.

❑ Don't discuss your cargo, destination, or the trip specifics on the CB or near strangers.

❑ If you believe you are being followed, call 911 and your dispatcher immediately.

❑ Avoid being boxed in on the road. Where possible leave room in front and behind your rig.

❑ Look for vehicles following you, especially if there are three or more people in the following vehicle.

❑ If you believe there is a threat of hijacking, notify your dispatcher and try to keep your rig moving.

When you stop your rig

❑ If you stop for a meal, try to stop where you can meet a buddy—or make sure someone in the parking area knows you, your rig, and how long you'll be parked.

❑ Leave your rig in a secure parking lot or truck stop. If not possible, be certain someone you trust can watch your rig.

❑ If team driving, always leave one person with the rig.

❑ Never leave your rig running with the keys in it. Instead, shut off the engine and lock the doors.

❑ If at all possible, do not stop in unsafe or high-crime areas. If you're in a strange destination, ask about the safest place to park your rig.

❑ Always lock the cargo door(s) with padlocks.

❑ Use trailer door seals to prevent and identify tampering.

Tractor-trailer security

The following are some additional steps to take (if you aren't taking them already) that will increase the security for your tractor-trailer rig whenever you have to stop, before going on the road, and while it is being loaded.

❑ Use an engine kill switch.

❑ Use tractor and trailer locking devices.

❑ Check your system often and notify the dispatcher if there is any type of malfunction in your system.

❑ If you drop a trailer, use a fifth wheel lock whenever possible.

Why is security so important?

It has been pointed out by Jeffery Beatty, security expert and president of Total Security Services International, that five highway trailers filled with explosives and parked in a city center would be able to do incredible damage.

Beatty suggests that food riots could break out if regular shipments were not able to move into grocery stores within several hours after an attack. "This would happen not because the shelves were bare but because the public would be insecure about what was going to happen next," he said, "and, therefore, the cost of a single large truck bomb incident could reach $5 billion—with government response driving the cost up by 10 times."

In devising a security plan, the American Trucking Associations (ATA) wants to deter terrorists and, most importantly, reduce vulnerability and ward off attacks. One of the most important parts of a security plan, according to the ATA, is putting the right person behind the wheel and that can be done with the proper background checks.

Other aspects of a security plan include load tracking, cargo security, and employee training—to do their jobs correctly while staying alert to terrorist threats or any unusual activity.

The centerpiece of the ATA security plan is training to:

❑ Know what to look for and where to be alert.

❑ Look at what's "vulnerable" and what is to be a "likely target."

❑ Detect operational acts—what terrorists do during their rehearsals—for example, in Oklahoma City, there were 140 "acts" of observing the building, observing traffic patterns, observing likely parking spots, etc.

❑ Know your fellow drivers.

❑ Know your neighbors in a parking lot.

❑ Know who is driving what rig.

Personnel security

❑ It is important to realize that any employee could pose a security risk—and identification procedures are a priority, especially for those employees leaving the company.

❑ Driver qualifications will be reviewed with special attention given to (1) gaps in employment, (2) frequent job changes, (3) all names used by applicant, (4) type of military discharge, (5) citizenship (present and prior residence information), (6) personal references, and (7) criminal history.

En route security

The following suggestions have been made to help drivers maintain security for themselves, their rigs, and their cargoes when they are over-the-road. These suggestions include:

❑ Avoid high population areas, including downtown or metropolitan areas, tunnels and bridges (See 49 CFR 397.67 at www.fmcsa.dot.gov)

❑ Ensure all hazardous materials are delivered as soon as possible.

❑ Drivers should always lock vehicles when in transit or when vehicles are left unattended.

❑ 49 CFR Part 397 provides rules for parking and attendance for vehicles. These should be reviewed.

❑ Drivers must be aware if a vehicle or vehicles are following their trucks.

❑ Drivers should also beware of strangers asking inappropriate questions about their rigs or their cargoes or their destinations.

❑ Drivers should be suspicious of individuals asking them to stop as a result of an alleged traffic accident. If unsure whether an accident has occurred, drive to a police station or well-lit, busy location before stopping.

❑ Be cautious about stopping to help stranded motorists or at accident scenes. The better route would be to call the State Police and report the stranded motorists or the accident, instead.

❑ DO NOT PICK UP HITCH HIKERS.

❑ Don't discuss the nature of your cargo over the CB radio, at coffee shops, truck stops, etc.

❑ Be aware of your surroundings at all times.

❑ Have the means to maintain communication with your company or dispatcher at all times. These means would include cell phones, two-way radios, CBs, satellite communications systems, etc.

❑ Be aware of the technology that could help you increase and improve your personal security and the security of your rig and your cargoes—such as cell phones, satellite tracking, and surveillance systems.

❑ Look for state-of-the-art locks and seals.

❑ Consider tamperproof locking features for fifth wheels—so trailer loads cannot be stolen.

❑ Consider installing electronic engine controls that require a code in addition to a key to start the vehicle.

❑ Consider theft-prevention devices, steering locks, fuel cutoff switches, electrical cutoff switches, and other high-security ignition devices.

As a professional driver, you should be aware that terrorist activities tend to occur in a series. If new attacks begin, tighten your security because of the possibilities of increased efforts on the part of terrorists.

It is also important to increase security measures whenever your nation, or a neighboring nation, is involved in military activities in foreign countries. Military involvement in a foreign land only invites retaliation from the terrorists bred in that country. It also gives terrorists, in general, a reason to heighten their efforts to attack your nation in as many ways as possible.

Finally, those suspicious activities you would have ignored two years ago now are good reasons to remain vigilant and report what you have observed. Not reporting suspicious activities that may lead to violence and death is more of a problem than reporting activities that may not lead to violence. Law enforcement does not mind following a lead that doesn't pan out . . . and it is much worse to miss warning signs that are costly in terms of lives and property.

Terrorism costs more than buildings. It costs lives, national confidence, and our ability to grow as a free nation. Protect yourself at all costs. Protect your rig and your cargo. It's a big part of the job!

WHAT ELSE CAN BE DONE?

Make yourself aware of technical innovations that assist in security

❑ Invest in cell phones, satellite tracking, and surveillance systems.

❑ Look at state-of-the-art seals and locks.

❑ Ensure access control systems are appropriate.

❑ Consider tamper-proof locking features for 5th wheels.

❑ Consider use of blanket-type alarms that signal when the blanket is moved.

❑ Consider installing electronic engine controls that require a code, in addition to a key, to start the vehicle.

Consider communications a big piece of any security plan

❑ Develop a communications network to share information with others in the industry.

❑ Develop a means of communication from office to vehicle.

While driving in the United States, call 9-1-1 for the following "emergencies"

❑ Life-threatening road conditions

❑ DWI and erratic driving

❑ Criminal activities, such as assaults, drug activity, etc.

❑ Vehicle accidents, including instances of hit and run

❑ Medical emergencies

❑ Unsafe equipment and insecure loads, which may endanger other drivers

❑ Life-threatening instances of road rage

❑ HazMat spills/accidents involving HazMat loads

❑ Any other life-threatening emergency witnessed by an observant driver

For non-emergencies, dial 1-855-TRUCKIN (878-2546)

❑ Hazardous road conditions—in all weather

❑ Closed roads/highways

❑ Abandoned vehicles

❑ Stolen vehicles

❑ Broken traffic signals

❑ Reckless or aggressive driving

❑ Excessive speed

❑ Stranded motorist

❑ Non-threatening debris on the highway, such as dead animals, wayward orange cones, car parts, and tire treads

❑ Congestion

Understand that terrorist activities tend to happen in groups—and if one attack occurs, heighten security immediately. Always increase security measures if the United States is engaged in military activity in a foreign country.

USING WIRELESS TELEPHONES SAFELY

(Courtesy of the Cellular Telecommunications Industry Association)

Wireless phones give professional drivers the ability to communicate by voice almost anywhere, anytime, and with anyone. Each year, American cell phone users make billions of calls, and these numbers are rapidly increasing. But, with this convenience comes an important responsibility—using good judgment at all times when making wireless calls.

The following tips will help make your wireless calls safer and less distracting if you must use your cell phone while you drive. However, it is important to note that while most professional drivers carry cell phones, rarely do any use these phones while they drive because of safety factors.

Safety tips include:

❑ Get to know your phone and its timesaving features, such as speed dial and redial. If you can, memorize the phone's keypad so you can use the speed dial function without taking your eyes off the road.

❑ Install a hands-free device if you can, and use a speaker phone whenever possible.

❑ Position your phone within easy reach and make sure you can grab it without taking your eyes off the road. If you get an incoming call at an inconvenient time, let your voice mail answer it for you.

❑ Stop any conversations during hazardous driving conditions or high traffic situations. As a professional driver, your first responsibility is to pay attention to the road.

❑ Don't try to take notes or directions or look up phone numbers or addresses while driving. Don't get caught in a dangerous situation because you are reading or writing and not paying attention to the road or other vehicles.

❑ Place as many calls as possible when you are not moving or before pulling into traffic. If you do need to make a call, dial a few numbers, check back on traffic and then complete dialing the number.

❑ Never get into a stressful or emotional conversation while you are driving. These kinds of conversations can be distracting and dangerous.

DEPARTMENT OF TRANSPORTATION RULES ON SECURITY REQUIREMENTS FOR CANADIAN TRUCK OPERATORS

(Information supplied by US-DOT Media Department)

The United States Department of Transportation (DOT) has issued temporary regulations (as of January 2003) that will provide for security checks of Canadian truck and rail operators carrying explosives to the United States to ensure that the operators do not pose a security risk.

Under the interim final rule (IFR) issued by the Transportation Security Administration (TSA), which has been posted at the *Federal Register* and published February 6, 2003, carriers of explosives from Canada to the United States by truck or rail must register with Transport Canada, the Canadian government agency responsible for transportation safety. Transport Canada will conduct checks to ensure that both the carriers and their customers who ship explosives are legitimate entities. Transport Canada also will check the drivers to ensure that they pose no security concerns. Transport Canada will then forward lists of approved carriers, shippers, and drivers to the TSA, which will make additional checks as appropriate and forward the lists to the United States Customs Service. Customs will allow Canadian explosives carriers to enter the United States only if the carrier, shipper, and operator are on the approved list.

The Safe Explosives Act, enacted in November 2002, added a number of categories of persons who may not lawfully transport explosives in interstate or foreign commerce without DOT authority, one of which was nonresident aliens. DOT issued the IFR under its authority to regulate the safety and security of transportation of hazardous materials. This action allows all legitimate Canadian carriers of explosives to operate their services into the United States without interruption.

The public will have 30 days to comment on the IFR, which is intended only as a temporary measure until the department completes consultations with Canada and other United States government agencies and issues more comprehensive regulations regarding background checks of persons transporting hazardous materials. DOT is also consulting with the government of Mexico to develop a similar system of security checks and will amend its rules to include Mexican explosives carriers in the near future.

The IFR and public comments are available on the Internet at http://dms.dot.gov docket number TSA-2003-14421.

CHAPTER 8

Driver Health and Safety

Fat Free Food

Salt Free Food

Cholesterol Free Food

Food Free Food

Cartoon by T. McCracken.

YOUR HEALTH

As a professional driver, one of your greatest challenges will be staying healthy. And staying healthy doesn't just mean eating the right diet, getting enough rest, getting exercise a few times a week, or avoiding stress. "Staying healthy" means doing all of these and anything else you can do to maintain good health, a positive outlook, and time for a satisfying career.

Today's drivers also need to avoid fatigue and "over-driving" whenever possible . . . and, although it goes without saying, it is worth mentioning that professional drivers should avoid using alcohol and drugs—at all costs.

In the year 2000, the estimated life expectancy of a United States citizen was close to 74 years. That number, of course, depends on the health habits of the individual.

A professional driver knows what has to be done to keep a truck running smoothly and to ensure a safe trip. Each part and each system contributes to keeping the vehicle operating safely.

The same principle is true for the body. To keep the body healthy and running smoothly, the driver must have—or develop—good eating habits, regular exercise, the proper amount of sleep, and he or she must also have a plan to manage stress.

Think of food as "fuel" for your body. Try to avoid foods high in fat content (an ounce of fat contains 2½ times the calories as an ounce of protein or carbohydrates). Avoid fried foods, and other foods that have a high fat content. Be mindful about eating too much salt and not eating enough vegetables and fruits or foods high in fiber.

In 2003, the Centers for Disease Control and Prevention reported that one-third of all United States citizens were candidates for diabetes, a disease that can be fairly well controlled with medication. The issue most people do not realize is that diabetes can lead to an onset of other medical complications such as high blood pressure, heart disease, and stroke, and if not treated, can end lives prematurely.

Diabetes, and the probability of becoming diabetic, may be controlled with low-fat, low-sugar diets, exercise, and maintaining a sensible weight.

Try to stay around 2000 calories per day for men and about 1600 calories per day for women.

Incorporating daily exercise

To keep your body running as smoothly as your rig, you must have a total exercise program. A total exercise program consists of movement, strength training, and development of flexibility.

Movement can be any activity that is done briskly. This includes walking, swimming, playing basketball, rope jumping, mowing the grass, hiking, playing golf, riding a stationary bike, or any number of other activities.

Walking is recommended because it requires no special facilities and no special equipment, only a pair of shoes, open space, and a professional driver trying to stay healthy.

Your safety

To become a safe and efficient driver—whether you drive domestically or internationally—it is important to be constantly aware of the over-the-road environment and what's going on around your rig at all times. For the international driver, this awareness is crucial, especially when driving in a new country for the first time. The driver will experience the additional stress of not knowing the highways, the terrain, or the customs of the country, be it Canada, the United States, or Mexico.

Every vehicle travels in two environments. One is the *external environment*, the environment outside the cab of the tractor that the driver constantly has to be aware of—using the senses of seeing, hearing, feeling, and sensing, while driving.

The *interior environment*—the environment in the cab of the tractor where the driver must be constantly aware of the conditions in which he has to work. The interior environment is important because the cab's environment has a great impact on how the driver feels, how quickly the driver is fatigued, and how well the driver can react to factors outside the cab. Is the temperature too hot or too cold? Are there exhaust fumes filtering into the cab? Is the clatter of the CB distracting? Is the music too loud and too chaotic?

All of these factors impact how you drive. These environments change every second your vehicle is moving. Therefore, the driver is constantly adjusting his awareness of what is going on around him.

From the driver's seat

Think about what you are able to see when you are behind the wheel of a big rig. The view from the tractor's cab is much different from the view you have when you are behind the wheel of your personal vehicle.

Obviously, you can see a greater distance ahead because you are sitting higher above the traffic. In some cases, you can see *over* the traffic, which is to your advantage!

On the flip side, you cannot see as well to the sides and rear of your rig as you can when you are driving your personal vehicle. In the cab of a tractor, it is difficult to see the right side of the tractor-trailer and along the drive wheels on both sides. And, behind the wheel of a big rig, it is also difficult to see smaller vehicles.

The professional driver must be able to get a clear, complete, and accurate picture of the external environment. Of course there are existing blind spots that cannot be eliminated unless the driver does a vehicle walk-around before getting into the truck and makes the needed adjustments.

For example, blind spots exist in the front of the tractor and at the rear of the trailer. To be eliminated, these must be observed and cleared by the driver just as he would make sure the direction the truck is going is clear before starting the engine.

Keeping the road ahead in sight

While most of this discussion may seem obvious to you, it is important to explore the responsibilities of a professional driver as he or she takes to the road.

Without question, looking up the highway as well as watching the road directly ahead and to the back and sides of your rig makes you aware of the environment around the truck. Steering toward an imaginary target or a reference point in the center of your lane of travel keeps you in your lane and aware of any possible problems up ahead. Having a target will keep you and your vehicle centered in the lane you're traveling.

Veteran truckers will tell you that a good rule of thumb is to have a target at least the distance you'll travel in the next 12 to 15 seconds. Another name for this is "eye lead time." In city driving, 12 seconds equals about one block ahead. On the open highway, 12 seconds ahead is about a quarter mile. If you cannot look ahead one block in the city or a quarter mile on the highway, slow down and be extra alert.

Looking this far ahead will give you time to:

❑ Identify any problems ahead.

❑ Prepare for these problems.

❑ Decide how you can drive defensively around the problem.

❑ Check anything that could keep you from making any changes in speed, direction, lane, etc.

❑ Take the right action to keep you, and others around you, safe.

Looking ahead 12 to 15 seconds and having enough visual lead time will allow you to react efficiently and safely, save fuel and time—because you will have fewer close calls, near misses, or accidents.

Scanning: The importance of the visual search

While it is important to have a 12–15 second visual lead time as you drive, be careful not to spend all of your time staring at the roadway ahead. Why? Because it is also important to know what is going on around your rig—to the sides, the back and, yes, even on top of your rig.

Once you've chosen a reference point on the road ahead, make a visual search and scan around the rest of your rig. So, the routine is this: Look 12–15 seconds ahead of the rig and on both sides of the roadway ahead. Now, quickly look away from your reference point ahead and scan both sides and the back of your rig before returning to the reference point.

When scanning, look for anything that can affect your travel path:

❑ People, on foot and in cars

❑ Traffic signs

❑ Debris on the highway

❑ Signals

❑ Slick spots or pot holes in the road

❑ Intersections

❑ Merging lanes

❑ Road shoulders

❑ Construction zones

❑ School zones

❑ Stopped vehicles

❑ Emergency situations

As you scan, always look for bailout areas, places you can use to avoid a crash.

Visual search is one of the most critical components in driver safety and efficiency. A systematic search begins with a walk around the vehicle every time it is driven, paying close attention to the space in front and to the rear of the vehicle.

The only way to eliminate front and rear blind spots is to first be aware that they are there. The driver sitting behind the steering wheel ALWAYS has a blind spot directly in front of the vehicle that can range 30 to 50 feet in distance. A blind spot existing directly behind a vehicle can range 200 feet in distance. An eight-foot wide trailer multiplied by the 200-foot distance could equal 1,600-feet of blind space. So, *always begin a visual search before entering the vehicle.*

THE IMPORTANCE OF DOT PHYSICALS EVERY TWO YEARS

Some drivers dread going to a physician for a Department of Transportation physical as required every two years. Some drivers even visit physicians who will do only a cursory examination. In fact, the DOT physical has often saved lives by finding drivers who are at risk for heart attacks, high blood pressure, seizures, and other problems—and offering remedies for these problems.

Professional drivers help themselves by having a thorough physical examination every two years by DOT-trained physicians, and then seeing a family doctor regularly as well. It is definitely a benefit to remain healthy and to head off major medical problems before they start.

APPENDICES

Drivers' Aids

APPENDIX A: UNITED STATES CUSTOMS FORMS, WHAT THEY ARE AND WHERE YOU CAN FIND THEM

All forms that are available for the United States Customs Web site can be found at www.customs.ustreas.gov

4455 Certificate of Registration: For those goods that will be exported temporarily for repair; United States Customs will inspect the goods on their return.

7512 Transportation Entry and Manifest of Goods Subject to Customs Inspection and Permit: If you are planning to clear your load inland, your trailer is not sealed, or you are moving goods in-bond, you will need either (or both) a 7512 or 7512C.

IT Bond: Combined forms for bonded shipments that are moving in transit.

T&E Bond: Combined forms for bonded shipments moving in transit and for subsequent export.

7525-V Shipper's Export Declaration needed for the following conditions: Entering Mexico to be stored and ultimately shipped to third countries that are not known at the time of export. Requires a United States Department of Justice Drug Enforcement Administration export declaration (21CFR, part 1313) subject to the International Traffic in Arms regulations; or requiring a validated license from the United States Department of Commerce.

7533 U.S. Inward Cargo Manifest: Required for all imports into the United States. This form should be completed by the shipper. If none is available, one can be completed by using the Bill of Lading.

A8B/7512B Canada/United States Transit Manifest: An interchangeable form that is also used for importing U.S. goods or Canadian goods moving through the United States. then back to Canada.

Exporter's Certificate of Origin: Article 502 of the NAFTA requires that an importer base his claims on the exporter's written certificate of origin. This may be the United States-approved CF 434, CERTIFICATE OF ORIGIN; the Canadian Certificate of Origin (Canadian Form B-232), or the Mexican Certificate of Origin (Certificado de Origen). This certificate may cover a single shipment or may be utilized as a blanket declaration for a period of 12 months. In either case, the certificate must be in the importer's possession when making the claim.

Bill of Lading (B/L): This document is one you should not leave without. You should have a B/L for each shipment in your load that describes in detail each shipment on your truck.

United States Customs Invoice, Commercial Invoice, Packing Slip: These documents provide the information needed to obtain the release of goods into the United States.

Pro-Forma Invoice: A company invoice printed on official company paper to represent the sale of goods to the purchaser. Also, needed for goods to be released into the United States.

NAFTA Certificate of Origin: Importers must provide United States Customs with a NAFTA Certificate of Origin for goods that qualify as originating under the North American Free Trade Agreement.

Mill Specification Certificate: Required if you are carrying primary steel; the shipper or manufacturer must give you this certificate. However, it is not required for steel products.

Special Export Licenses: Some goods like defense and technological equipment require special export license that needs to be completed by the shipper and given to United States Customs.

"Trukin' down the road
I drink 20 cups of coffee a day
I can fill out a 1000 forms an hour
But the wait is long
So I write them songs
'cause I'm done with the forms . . . "

Cartoon by T. McCracken.

APPENDIX B: CANADIAN CUSTOMS FORMS, WHAT THEY ARE AND WHERE YOU CAN FIND THEM

All forms are available at the CCRA Web site at www.ccra-adrc.gc.ca.

A8A or A8A(B) Cargo Control Document (CCD): The carrier's report to Customs. It is either the carrier's or driver's responsibility to complete.

Manifest: Interchangeable form for importing United States goods or Canadian goods moving through the United States, then back to Canada.

B13 or B13A Export Declaration: Only necessary for goods that will leave Canada.

Bill of Lading (B/L): The document a driver should not leave the dock without. You should have a B/L for each shipment in your load that describes in detail each shipment on your truck.

Canada Customs Invoice, Commercial Invoice, Packing Slip: These documents provide the information needed to obtain the release of goods into Canada. There are three invoicing options:

❑ Canada Customs Invoice (CCI), which either you or the vendor can complete (for instructions on how to complete the CCI, see Memorandum *D1-4-1*, Canada Customs Invoice Requirements at www.ccra-adrc.gc.ca/E/pub/cm/d1-4-1);

❑ A commercial invoice containing the same information as a CCI; or

❑ A commercial invoice, which indicates the buyer, seller, country of origin, price paid or payable, and a detailed description of the goods, including quantity, and a CCI that provides the remaining information.

Pro-Forma Invoice: A company invoice printed on official company paper to represent the sale of goods to the purchaser. Also, needed for goods to be released into Canada.

Canadian Waste Manifest: If any shipment contains hazardous wastes, you must give photocopies of the Canadian Waste Manifest to Canada Customs, along with a "Notice/Transit Notice" form and a letter to proceed, or a written confirmation letter. Make sure you always keep the original for the extent of your trip; give photocopies to Customs.

E15 Certificate of Export: If any of the shipments you are carrying need to be examined prior to their departure from Canada, they must be presented to Customs for certification along with an E15 document.

E29B Temporary Admission Permit Necessary Document: If anything in a load of freight is being temporarily imported into Canada and later exported. For example, items needing to be repaired or used in a show or performance. A security deposit or bond equal to the amount of duties and taxes that would be charged if the goods were to be imported may be demanded by Canada Customs.

NAFTA Certificate of Origin: Importers must provide Canada Customs with a NAFTA Certificate of Origin for goods that qualify as originating under the North American Free Trade Agreement.

APPENDIX C: MEXICAN CUSTOMS FORMS, WHAT THEY ARE AND WHERE YOU CAN FIND THEM

All forms must be completed in Spanish or, if available only in English, a Spanish translation must accompany all forms.

Forms validating the driver, his or her rig, and the carrier that employs the driver. These are available from the SCT and include (1) DGTT-No1 (Solicitud de permiso para el autotransporte federal) and (2) DGTT-N20 (Declaracion de caracteristicas y estado fisico de vehiculos de cargo).

Other forms required by Customs at the Mexican Border include: (1) The Assignment Letter, (2) Bill of Lading, (3) Packing Slip, (4) Composition Analysis, (5) Invoice, (6) Labelling Waiver Declaration, (7) NAFTA Certificate of Origin, (8) NOM Certificates (standards), (9) Phytosanitary Certificate, and (10) Serial Number List.

APPENDIX D: INSURANCE INFORMATION FROM THE TRI-NATIONAL INSURANCE COMMITTEE

Under the North American Free Trade Agreement (NAFTA), one area requiring further study has been the lack of standardized commercial insurance requirements in the three countries. This lack has created some difficulties in free trade and has impeded the free flow of commercial traffic across the borders.

A trilateral working group comprised of insurance associations, regulators, and transport officials, was established to identify insurance issues for cross-border trucking. A trilateral discussion on how to harmonize cross-border trucking insurance requirements was revitalized in 2001 and the NAFTA Tri-national Insurance Working Group, operating under the Financial Services Committee, continues to meet to discuss feasible options toward insurance compatibility. Short- and long-term objectives and options are being reviewed, with the ultimate objective identified as being mutual recognition: one insurance policy recognized by authorities in all three countries.

In this context, one option for the provision of cross-border trucking insurance is the Canadian Power of Attorney and Undertaking (PAU) system.

Under this system, Canadian and United States insurance companies can enter into business arrangements for the provision of seamless insurance coverage for commercial vehicles operating across the border. The PAU system, which responded to a need for a common proof of insurance coverage for the many U.S. drivers entering Canada, denotes compliance with minimum insurance coverage requirements.

However, due to varying provincial motor carrier licensing requirements, it is common for United States insurers to enter into a "fronting" arrangement with a Canadian insurer, whereby the United States insurer does the underwriting on the United States truck and issues the policy in the Canadian insurer's name, and the Canadian insurer "reinsures" the risk back to the United States insurer.

The provision of commercial insurance coverage for southbound Canadian carriers operating in the United States is somewhat similar. To gain entry into the United States, a Canadian trucker must file certificates of financial responsibility and have proof of insurance. A Canadian insurer enters into an arrangement with an American insurer under which the United States insurer does the necessary filings for the Canadian carrier and provides proof of insurance and the United States insurer "reinsures" the risk back to the Canadian insurer.

The ongoing recognition by Canada and the United States of each other's insurance policies has been effective due to similarities in the insurance, regulatory, and legal environments in the two countries. Most goods shipped from Mexico into the United States are protected by trip insurance. However, continuous insurance is expected to become the norm once the southern border opens up.

Mexico's federal government, in cooperation with state governments, sets the minimum insurance requirements for motor carriers. Under NAFTA, foreign insurance companies can now operate subsidiaries in Mexico to provide (limited) insurance services. There are no more restrictions on foreign ownership of Mexican-based insurance companies. However, Mexico still maintains its NAFTA reservation on the provision of third-party liability coverage within Mexico; it can only be provided by Mexican-domiciled and registered insurers. Texas insurance law maintains the same third-party liability restriction on the provision of insurance to Mexican carriers.

Recognizing that true insurance mutual recognition would require at least two national governments to change existing insurance regulations, this is likely more of a long-term objective. A number of more feasible, short-term alternatives under existing laws and insurance regulations are being discussed by the NAFTA Trilateral Insurance Working Group:

❑ **Brokered Arrangements:** Managing General Agents (MGAs) are well established at southern border locations and represent both American and Mexican insurance companies selling coverage to cross-border traffic. The system works fairly well, but requires two separate (back-to-back) policies. MGAs typically arrange advance coverage for carriers for cross-border movement in 12-month intervals.

❑ **Joint Ventures:** Seen as an outgrowth of brokered arrangements, these are contractual arrangements between insurers to combine coverages and provide seamless insurance (one company "fronts," or issues policies on behalf of the other company).

❑ **Multinational Insurance Companies:** As large multinationals (i.e., Zurich Insurance) can now own 100% of a Mexican-based subsidiary, they are well positioned to provide coverage in more than one country and work with domiciled insurers to accommodate domestic insurance regulations (i.e., Mexico's third-party liability reservation).

❑ **Fronting Arrangements:** An arrangement whereby a domestic insurer takes on the risk of a foreign insurance company and issues a policy on behalf of the foreign insurer. This system is very common, where Canadian insurers enter into business arrangements (or joint ventures) with United States companies that front coverage to southbound Canadian carriers. The United States company issues an insurance certificate for the Canadian carrier but doesn't necessarily want to underwrite the risk, so "re-insures," or transfers the risk back to the Canadian insurer.

❑ **Canadian Power of Attorney and Undertaking (PAU):** This system, or a system similar to it, as described earlier, is being considered for broader application, encompassing the United States-Mexico border.

APPENDIX E: NORTH AMERICAN FREE TRADE AGREEMENT— UNITED STATES DEPARTMENT OF TRANSPORTATION REGULATIONS   (Provided by FMCSA—March, 2002)

❑ Regulations issued in March 2002 explain how Mexican-domiciled carriers may apply for operating authority beyond the United States-Mexico border commercial zones. The rules include requirements that meet the terms of the Transportation and Related Agencies Appropriations Act, 2002.

❑ Mexican-domiciled carriers and United States and Canadian carriers are governed by the same safety standards when operating in the United States.

❑ Mexican-domiciled carriers applying to operate to and from the United States are required to have a distinctive USDOT number, undergo safety monitoring initially and during an 18-month provisional period.

❑ During operations under provisional operating authority, and for 36 months after receiving permanent authority, Mexican vehicles operating beyond the border commercial zones into the United States must display a valid Commercial Vehicle Safety Alliance inspection decal.

❑ The regulations require all Mexican-domiciled carriers entering the United States to have a drug and alcohol-testing program, a system of compliance with United States federal hours-of-service requirements, adequate data and safety management systems, and valid insurance with a United States registered insurance company.

❑ Mexican commercial vehicles with authority to operate beyond the commercial zones will be permitted to enter the United States only at commercial border crossings and only when a certified motor carrier safety inspector is on duty.

❑ Federal and state safety inspectors will be required to inspect and verify the status and validity of the license of each driver of a long-haul Mexican-domiciled motor carrier (1) when carrying a placardable quantity of hazardous material, (2) when undergoing a full vehicle driver Commercial Vehicle Safety Alliance inspection, and (3) 50 percent of other long-haul Mexican drivers engaged in cross-border operations.

❑ Mexican-domiciled carriers planning to operate solely within the commercial zones along the United States-Mexico border will be required, within 18 months, to apply for provisional Certificates of Registration, which grant temporary authority to operate in the United States. The provisional Certificate of Registration cannot be made permanent for at least 18 months, until the carrier has successfully completed a safety audit.

❑ DOT will provide all Mexican-domiciled carriers educational and technical assistance before the restrictions on Mexican carrier operations are lifted.

❑ DOT and States will also do the following:

   ❑ Equip all United States-Mexico commercial border crossings with scales suitable for enforcement action.

   ❑ Equip five of the ten locations with the highest volume of commercial vehicle crossings with weigh-in-motion (WIM) scales before reviewing or processing carrier applications beyond the border zones. Three are operational (Otay Mesa, Nogales, Bridge of Americas/El Paso) and two more (Columbia-Solidarity Bridge/Laredo and Eagle Pass, Texas) should be in place by April 1, 2003.

❑ Equip the remaining five of the highest volume of commercial vehicle crossings (World Trade Bridge/Laredo; Pharr, Texas; Veterans' Bridge/Brownsville; Calexico, Calif. and Ysleta/El Paso) with weigh-in-motion devices within 12 months. An additional five will be in place by December 2002.

NAFTA—Truck and bus provisions

❑ Approved by Congress in 1993 and entered into force in 1994, the North American Free Trade Agreement was based on a simple premise—that all of the countries in North America would be integrated into one free trade area.

❑ Under NAFTA's original timeline, the United States and Mexico agreed to permit access to each other's border states by December 18, 1995. Reciprocal access beyond the border states was promised by January 1, 2000. (Canadian carriers have been operating throughout the United States since 1982.)

❑ The NAFTA timetable also called for the United States and Mexico to lift all restrictions on regular route, scheduled cross-border bus service by January 1, 1997.

❑ In December 1995, President Clinton postponed implementation of the NAFTA cross-border trucking provision, which continued to limit Mexican trucks to operations in designated commercial zones within Arizona, California, New Mexico, and Texas.

APPENDIX F: NEW RULES CONCERNING THE UNITED STATES COMMERCIAL DRIVING LICENSE   (Provided by FMCSA)

In July, 2002, the Federal Motor Carrier Safety Administration released new rules covering the Commercial Driver's License that went into effect September 30 of that same year. The new rules that became part of the Motor Carrier Safety Improvement Act of 1999 include tougher penalties on drivers and states that do not comply with the provisions of the Act.

Basically, the Motor Carrier Safety Improvement Act of 1999 amended Title 49 of the United States Code relating to the licensing and sanctioning of commercial motor vehicle drivers required to hold a CDL, and directed the DOT to amend its regulations to correct specific weaknesses in the CDL program.

The possible benefits expected from the new rules include fewer CDL-related fatal crashes and fatalities because of the additional CMV operators and CDL holders, specifically, who will be suspended or disqualified for violation of the new disqualifying offenses and serious traffic violations covered under this rule.

The new rules state that a commercial driver can be disqualified if the driver's non-commercial license has been cancelled, revoked, or suspended as a result of convictions for traffic violations when driving a passenger vehicle. Disqualification can also occur if the driver has committed drug or alcohol-related offenses while driving a passenger vehicle.

New disqualifying offenses include driving a commercial vehicle with a suspended or revoked CDL and causing a fatality through negligent driving in either a CMV or a passenger vehicle.

States failing to comply with FMCSA's guidelines on issuing licenses and maintaining proper legal databases will risk losing federal funding as well as the right to issue CDLs. If this occurs, drivers operating in that state will be forced to go to another state to get a non-resident CDL.

The new CDL rules include the following specific directives (1999):

❏ Seven new provisions in the regulation address the following: disqualification for driving while suspended, disqualified, or causing a fatality; emergency disqualification of drivers posing an imminent hazard; expanded definition of serious traffic violations; extended driver record check; new notification requirements; masking prohibition; disqualification for violations obtained while driving a noncommercial motor vehicle.

❏ The Motor Carrier Safety Improvement Act of 1999 requires the agency to withhold Motor Carrier Safety Assistance Program grant funds from the states if they do not comply with the regulation.

❏ A new masking prohibition does not prevent a conviction from appearing on a driver's record and requires making conviction information available to authorized parties.

❏ Applicants for an initial CDL, and those transferring or renewing a CDL, must provide state driver licensing agency personnel with the name of all states where previously licensed for the past ten years to drive any type of motor vehicle, allowing state officials to obtain an applicant's complete driving record. The final rule limits this record check to CDL drivers initially renewing their license after the effective date of this rulemaking.

❏ States must maintain a CDL driver-history record noting an individual's convictions for state or local motor-vehicle traffic-control laws while operating any type of motor vehicle. Information on these convictions and other licensing actions must be kept a minimum of three years. Disqualifying offenses range from three years to life.

❏ The Federal Motor Carrier Safety Administration (FMCSA) may prohibit a state from issuing, renewing, transferring, or upgrading CDLs if the agency determined the state is in substantial noncompliance with the CDL licensing and sanctioning requirements.

❏ Under the new regulation, a driver may apply for a CDL from another state if the state he/she lives in was decertified and if the other state to which he/she applies elects to issue that license. States are authorized, but not required, to issue nonresident CDLs to such drivers.

❏ The regulations add these serious traffic violations: driving a CMV without obtaining a CDL; driving a CMV without a CDL in the driver's possession; and driving a CMV without the proper CDL and/or endorsement. Driver disqualification can result if a driver is convicted two or more times within a three-year period.

❏ States must be connected to the CDLIS and the National Driver Register (NDR) to exchange information about CMV drivers and traffic convictions and disqualifications. A state must check CDLIS, NDR, and the current State of licensure before a CDL can be issued, renewed, upgraded, or transferred to make sure the driver is not disqualified or has a license from more than one state. Employers, including motor carriers, are authorized users of CDLIS data and, therefore, have access to an employee's or an applicant's driving record.

❏ New notification requirements necessitate that states inform CDLIS and the state issuing the CDL no later than 10 days after disqualifying, revoking, suspending, or canceling a CDL, or refusing to allow someone for at least 60 days to operate a CMV. Beginning three years after the final rule's effective date, notification of traffic-violation convictions must occur within 30 days of the conviction. Six years after the final rule's effective date, notification of traffic-violation convictions must occur within ten days of the conviction.

❏ States whose CDL program may fail to meet compliance requirements, but are making a "good-faith effort" to comply with the CDL requirements, are eligible to receive emergency CDL grants.

❏ The FMCSA decided to merge all the CDL provisions into one final rule with one effective date because they were so closely related to one another.

APPENDIX G: UNITED STATES DOT SAFETY RULES FOR LOAD SECUREMENT

D.O.T. out-of-service criteria for load management

The following are points covered by roadside inspectors regarding how cargoes are loaded and those loading errors that could cause a rig to be put out-of-service:

❏ Spare tire or portion of load/dunnage could fall from vehicle.

❏ Improperly latched fitting for securing container to container chassis solely via corner fittings (for intermodal freight).

❏ 25 percent or more of type/number of tie-downs required by Federal Motor Carrier Safety Regulation 393.102 are loose or missing.

❏ 25 percent or more of required type/number of tie-downs are defective.

❏ Chain is defective if working portion contains knot or damaged/deformed/worn links. Clevis-type repair link, if as strong as original link, is okay.

❏ Wire rope is defective if working portion contains: kinked, bird-caged or pitted section; over three broken wires in any strand; over two broken wires at fitting; over 11 broken wires in any length measuring six times its diameter (for instance, with 1/2-inch thick rope, more than 11 broken wires in any three-inch section); repairs other than back/eye splice; discoloration from heat or electric arc.

❏ Fiber rope is defective if working portion contains: burned/melted fibers, except on heat-sealed ends; excessive wear, reducing diameter 20 percent; any repair (properly spliced lengths are not considered a repair); ineffective (easily loosened) knot used for connection/repair.

❏ Synthetic webbing is defective if working portion contains: knot; more than 25 percent of stitches separated; broken/damaged hardware; any repair or splice; overt damage; severe abrasion; cumulative for entire working length of one strap, cuts/burns/holes exceeding width of 3/4 inch for 4-inch wide webbing, exceeding width of 5/6 inch for 3-inch wide webbing or exceeding width of 3/8 inch for 1-3/4-inch wide or 2-inch wide webbing. Multiple defects confined to one strand of a strap are not cumulative (just measure largest single defect in that strand).

❏ Load binders or fittings that obviously are cracked, worn, corroded, distorted or discolored from heat or electric arc.

❏ Evidence of wire rope slipping through cable clamp.

❏ Anchor point on vehicle displays: distorted/cracked rails or supports; cracked weld; damaged/worn floor rings.

Tarps

Tarps will be needed to protect much of the cargo you haul. Tarps should cover the maximum load, measuring 8 ft. × 14 ft. × 42 ft.

Worn tarps or tarps with holes offer little or no protection. Make sure you inspect your tarps regularly and ensure that they are functional.

If you don't have enough tarps to protect your load, contact your driver manager. It is always better to buy protection with tarping than to pay a damage claim.

Do not secure the edges of tarps to the outside of the trailer rub rail. This allows grime and moisture to get under the tarp.

Caution: Winds can be very dangerous when installing tarps, so always: (1) consider the wind direction, (2) consider the strength of the wind or expected gusts, (3) secure tarps in a sequence that minimizes risk, and (4) get help and avoid injury.

Note: Loads of plastic pipe always require a smoke tarp covering the forward openings.

Tarping rules

- ❏ When tarping is required—tarp! Failure to tarp moisture-sensitive freight could result in termination with some companies.

- ❏ Before going to a shipper to load tarped freight, make certain your tarps are in good condition and not full of holes. If so, they should be replaced.

- ❏ The best way to take care of your tarps is to pad EACH and EVERY sharp and protruding object.

- ❏ Use carpet, old straps, or rubber mud flap along with duct tape to hold padding in place.

- ❏ A good tarp job does not consist of simply throwing on the tarp, applying a few ropes, and going down the road. It takes time, skill, labor, and careful planning.

If your tarped load has multiple stops and it is raining, check with your driver manager before you untarp if you are not going to be unloaded inside or under cover. Damage could result to your other freight, possibly causing a costly claim.

APPENDIX H: EMBASSIES AND CONSULATES

Consulate Generals of Canada in the United States

Canadian Embassy
501 Pennsylvania Avenue, N.W.
Washington, D.C. 20001
Tel: (202) 682-1740

One CNN Center
South Tower, Suite 400
Atlanta, Georgia 30303-2705
Tel: (404) 577-6810

3 Copley Place
Suite 400
Boston, Massachusetts 02116
Tel: (617) 262-3760

1 Marine Midland Center
Suite 3000
Buffalo, New York 14203-2884
Tel: (716) 858-9500

Two Prudential Plaza
180 North Stetson Avenue
Suite 2400
Chicago, Illinois 60601
Tel: (312) 616-1860

St. Paul Place
750 North St. Paul Street
Suite 1700
Dallas, Texas 75201-3247
Tel: (214) 922-9806

600 Renaissance Center
Suite 1100
Detroit, Michigan 48243-1798
Tel: (313) 567-2340

300 South Grand Avenue
10th Floor
Los Angeles, California 90071
Tel: (213) 687-7432

200 South Biscayne Boulevard
Suite 1600
Miami, Florida 33131
Tel: (305) 579-1600

701 4th Avenue South
Minneapolis, Minnesota 55415
Tel: (612) 333-4641

1251 Avenue of the Americas
16th Floor
New York, New York 10020-1175
Tel: (212) 596-1600

412 Plaza 600
Sixth and Stewart
Seattle, Washington 98101-1286
Tel: (206) 443-1777

Canadian Consulates in Mexico

Canadian Embassy
Consular Section
Calle Schiller No. 529
Col. Bosque de Chapultepec
Del. Miguel Hidalgo
C.P. 11580, Mexico D.F.
Tel: +52 (55) 5724-7900
Fax: +52 (55) 5724-7943

Consular Emergencies Outside Office Hours: Contact the Watch Office free of charge, 24 hours a day, seven days a week by telephoning:

- ❑ (613) 996-8885 (collect via Canada Direct) or

- ❑ the Embassy at +52 (55) 5724-7900 or if you are outside of Mexico City dial 01-800-706-2900 (press "0")

Centro Comercial Marbella, Local 23
Prolongación Farallón s/n, esq. Miguel Alemán
39690 Acapulco, Guerrero
Tel: (744) 484-1305
Fax: (744) 484-1306
E-mail: acapulco@canada.org.mx

Plaza Caracol II
3er piso, local 330, Blvd. Kukulkán km.8.5
Zona Hotelera
77500, Cancún, Quintana Roo
Tel: (998) 883-3360
Fax: (998) 883-3232
E-mail: cancun@canada.org.mx

Hotel Fiesta Americana Local 31,
Aurelio Aceves 225, Sector Juárez
44100 Guadalajara, Jalisco
Tel: (33) 3615-6215
Fax: (33) 3615-8665
E-mail: gjara@dfait-maeci.gc.ca

Avenida Playa Gaviotas, # 202
Zona Dorada,
82110, Mazatlán, Sinaloa
Tel: (669) 913-7320
Fax: (669) 914-6655
E-mail: mazatlan@canada.org.mx

Schiller 529
Col. Polanco (Rincón del Bosque)
11580 México, D.F.
MEXICO

Edificio Kalos
Piso C-1, Local 108-A
Zaragoza 1300 Sur y Constitución
06400 Monterrey, Nuevo León
Tel: (81) 8344-2753, 3200
Fax: (81) 8344-3048
E-mail: mntry@dfait-maeci.gc.ca

Pino Suarez 700
Local 11 B
Multiplaza Brena, Col. Centro
68000 Oaxaca, Oaxaca
Tel: (951) 513-3777
Fax: (951) 515-2147
E-mail: oaxaca@canada.org.mx

Calle Zaragoza #160, Interior 10
Colonia Centro,
48300 Puerto Vallarta, Jalisco
Tel: (322) 222-5398/0858
Fax: (322) 222-3517
E-mail: vallarta@canada.org.mx

Plaza José Green, local 9
Blvd Mijares s/n
Col. Centro
23400 San José del Cabo, B.C.S.
Tel: (624) 142-4333
Fax: (624) 142-4262
E-mail: loscabos@canada.org.mx

Germán Gedovius no. 10411-101,
Condominio del Parque, Zona Rió
22320, Tijuana, Baja California Norte
Tel: (664) 684-0461
Fax: (664) 684-0301
E-mail: tijuana@canada.org.mx

Mexican Consulates in the United States

ARIZONA

1201 F Avenue
Douglas, AZ 85607
Tel: (520) 364-3142
Fax: (520) 364-1379

571 N. Grand Ave.
Nogales, AZ 85621
Tel: (520) 287-2521
Fax: (520) 287-3175

1990 W. Camelback, Suite 110
Phoenix, AZ 85015
Tel: (602) 242-7398
Fax: (602) 242-2957

553 S. Stone Ave.
Tuscon, AZ 85701
Tel: (520) 882-5595
Fax: (520) 882-8959

CALIFORNIA

331 W. Second St.
Calexico, CA 92231
Tel: (760) 357-3863
Fax: (760) 357-6284

830 Van Ness Ave.
Fresno, CA 93721
Tel: (209) 233-9770
Fax: (209) 233-5838

2401 W. Sixth St.
Los Angeles, CA 90057
Tel: (213) 351-6800
Fax: (213) 389-9249
www.consulmex-la.com

201 E. Fourth St., Suite 206-A
Oxnard, CA 93030
Tel: (805) 483-4684
Fax: (805) 385-3527

1010 8th St.
Sacramento, CA 95814
Tel: (916) 441-3287
Fax: (916) 441-3176
E-mail: consulsac1@quiknet.com
www.quiknet.com/mexico

532 North D St.
San Bernadino, CA 92401
Tel: (909) 889-9837
Fax: (909) 889-8285

1549 India St.
San Diego, CA 92101
Tel: (619) 231-8414
Fax: (619) 231-4802
E-mail: info@consulmexsd.org
www.sre.gob.mx/sandiego

870 Market St. Suite 528
San Francisco, CA 94102
Tel: (415) 782-9555
Fax: (415) 392-3233
www.consulmexsf.com

540 North First St.
San Jose, CA 95112
Tel: (408) 294-3414
Fax: (408) 294-4506

828 N. Broadway St.
Santa Ana, CA 92701-3424
Tel: (714) 835-3069
Fax: (714) 835-3472

COLORADO

48 Steele St.
Denver, CO 80206
Tel: (303) 331-1110
Fax: (303) 331-0169

DISTRICT OF COLUMBIA

2827 16th Street, N.W.
Washington, D.C. 20009-4260
Tel: (202) 736-1000
Fax: (202) 234-4498 or 728-1750

FLORIDA

5975 Sunset Drive
South Miami, Florida 33143
Tel: (786) 268-4900
Fax: (786) 268-4895
E-mail: conmxmia@bellsouth.net
www.sre.gob.mx/miami

100 W. Washington St.
Orlando, FL 32801
Tel: (407) 422-0514
Fax: (407) 422-9633

GEORGIA

2600 Apple Valley Rd.
Atlanta, GA 30319
Tel: (404) 266-2233
Fax: (404) 266-2302

ILLINOIS

300 N. Michigan Ave., 2nd Fl.
Chicago, IL 60651
Tel: (312) 855-1380
Fax: (312) 855-9257

LOUISIANA

World Trade Center Building
2 Canal St., Suite 840
New Orleans, LA 70115
Tel: (504) 522-3596
Fax: (504) 525-2332

MASSACHUSETTS

20 Park Plaza, Suite 506
Boston, MA 02116
Tel: (617) 426-4181
Fax: (617) 695-1957
www.sre.gob.mx/boston

MICHIGAN

645 Griswold Ave., Suite 1770
Detroit, MI 48226
Tel: (313) 964-4515
Fax: (313) 567-7543

MISSOURI

1015 Locust St., Suite 922
Saint Louis, MO 63101
Tel: (314) 436-3233
Fax: (314) 436-2695

NEW MEXICO

400 Gold SW, Suite 100
Albuquerque, NM 87102
Tel: (505) 247-2139
Fax: (505) 842-9490

NEW YORK

27 East 39th St.
New York, NY 10016
Tel: (212) 217-6400
Fax: (212) 217-6493
www.consulmexny.org

NORTH CAROLINA

P.O. Box 19627
Charlotte, NC 28219
Tel. (704) 394-2190

OREGON

1234 S.W. Morrison
Portland, OR 97205
Tel: (503) 274-1450
Fax: (503) 274-1540

PENNSYLVANIA

111 S. Independence Mall East
Bourse Building, Suite 1010
Philadelphia, PA 19403
Tel: (215) 922-3834
Fax: (215) 923-7281

TEXAS

200 E. Sixth St., Suite 200
Austin, TX 78701
Tel: (512) 478-2866
Fax: (512) 478-8008
www.onr.com/consulmx

724 E. Elizabeth St.
Brownsville, TX 78520
Tel: (956) 542-4431
Fax: (956) 542-7267

800 N. Shoreline Blvd.
Suite 410, North Tower
Corpus Christi, TX 78401
Tel: (512) 882-3375
Fax: (512) 882-9324

8855 N. Stemmons Freeway
Dallas, TX 75247
Tel: (214) 630-7341
Fax: (214) 630-3511
www.consulmexdallas.com

300 E. Losoya
Del Rio, TX 78841
Tel: (830) 775-2352
Fax: (830) 774-6497

140 Adams St.
Eagle Pass, TX 78852
Tel: (830) 773-9255
Fax: (830) 773-9397

910 E. San Antonio St.
El Paso, TX 79901
Tel: (915) 533-3644
Fax: (915) 532-7163

10103 Fondren Rd., Suite 555
Houston, TX 77096
Tel: (713) 271-6800
Fax: (713) 271-3201
www.mexico-info.com

1612 Farragut St.
Laredo, TX 78040
Tel: (956) 723-6369
Fax: (956) 723-1741

600 S. Broadway Ave.
McAllen, TX 78501
Tel: (956) 686-0243
Fax: (956) 686-4901

511 W. Ohio, Suite 121
Midland, TX 79701
Tel: (915) 687-2334
Fax: (915) 687-3952

127 Navarro St.
San Antonio, TX 78205
Tel: (210) 271-9728
Fax: (210) 227-1817
www.hotx.com/consulado

UTAH

230 West 400 South
2nd Floor
Salt Lake City, Utah 84047
Tel: (801) 521-8502
Fax: (801) 521-0534

WASHINGTON

2132 Third Ave.
Seattle, WA 98121
Tel: (206) 448-3526
Fax: (206) 448-4771
www.sre.gob.mx/seattle

Mexican Consulates in Canada

BRITISH COLUMBIA

810–1130 W. Pender St.
Vancouver, B.C. VGE 4A4
Tel: (604) 684-3547
Fax: (604) 684-2485

ONTARIO

199 Bay St., Suite 4440
Commerce Court West
Toronto, Ont. M5L 1E9
Tel: (416) 368-8490
Fax: (416) 368-8342

QUEBEC

2000 Mansfield St., Suite 1015
Montreal, Que. H3A 2Z7
Tel: (514) 288-2502
Fax: (514) 288-8287

United States Consulates in Mexico

Ciudad Juarez
Avenida Lopez Mateos 924-N
Tel: (52) (656) 611-3000

Guadalajara
Progreso 175
Tel: (52) (333) 825-2998

Hermosillo
Avenida Monterrey 141
Tel: (52) (662) 217-2375

Matamoros
Avenida Primera 2002
Tel: (52) (868) 812-4402

Merida
Paseo Montejo 453
Tel: (52) (999) 925-5011

Monterrey
Avenida Constitucion 411
Poniente 64000
Tel: (52) (818) 345-2120

Nogales
Calle San Jose
Nogales, Sonora
Tel: (52) (631) 313-4820

Nuevo Laredo
Calle Allende 3330
Col. Jardin
Tel: (52) (867) 714-0512

Tijuana
Tapachula 96
Tel: (52) (664) 622-7400

United States Consular Agencies

Acapulco
Hotel Continental Plaza
Costera Miguel Aleman 121—Local 14
Tel: (52) (744) 484-03-00 or (52) (744) 469-0556

Cabo San Lucas
Blvd. Marina y Pedregal #1
Local No. 3, Zona Centro
Tel: (52) (624) 143-3566

Cancun
Plaza Caracol Two
Third Level, No. 320-323
Boulevard Kukulcan, km. 8.5, Zona Hotelera
Tel: (52) (998) 883-0272

Ciudad Acuna
Ocampo #305
Col. Centro
Tel: (52) (877) 772-8661
Fax: (52) (877) 772-8179

Cozumel
Plaza Villa Mar in the Main Square—El Centro
2nd floor right rear,
Locale #8, Avenida Juarez and 5th Ave. Norte
Tel: (52) (987) 872-4574

Ixtapa/Zihuatanejo
Local 9, Plaza Ambiente
Tel: (52) (755) 553-2100

Mazatlan
Hotel Playa Mazatlan
Rodolfo T. Loaiza #202
Zona Dorada
Tel: (52) (669) 916-5889

Oaxaca
Macedonio Alcala No. 407, Interior 20
Tel: (52) (951) 514-3054 or (52) (951) 516-2853

Piedras Negras
Prol. General Cepeda No. 1900
Fraccionamiento Privada Blanca, C.P. 26700
Tel: (52) (878) 785-1986

Puerto Vallarta
Edif. Vallarta, Plaza Zaragoza 160-Piso 2 Int-18
Tel: (52) (322) 222-0069

Reynosa
Calle Monterrey #390
Con Sinaloa, Colonia Rodriguez
Tel: (52) (899) 923-9331

San Luis Potosi
Edificio "Las Terrazas"
Avenida Venustiano Carranza 2076-41
Tel: (52) (444) 811-7802

San Miguel de Allende
Dr. Hernandez Macias #72
Tel: (52) (415) 152-2357 or (52) (415) 152-0068

United States Consulates in Canada

Information and requirements for obtaining United States passports, citizenship, and visas (including immigrant and non-immigrant) may be obtained in Canada by calling 1-900-451-2778, or residents in the United States may call 1-900-443-3131, or by visiting the website www.amcits.com.

The Embassy of the United States of America
490 Sussex Drive
Ottawa, Ontario K1N 1G8 Canada
Tel: (613) 238-5335

Office of Public Affairs
490 Sussex Drive
Ottawa, Ontario K1N 1G8 Canada
Tel: (613) 238-5335
Public Affairs does not provide visa or immigration information.

Consular Service
490 Sussex Drive
Ottawa, Ontario K1N 1G8 Canada
Tel: (613) 238-5335

Consulate General Calgary
615 Macleod Trail S.E., Room 1000
Calgary, Alberta, T2G 4T8

Consulate General Halifax
Suite 904, Purdy's Wharf Tower II
1969 Upper Water Street
Halifax, NS B3J 3R7

Consulate General Montréal
1155 St. Alexandre Street
Montréal, Québec H3B 1Z1
Mailing address:
Post Office Box 65
Postal Station Desjardins
Montréal, Québec H5B 1G1
Email: Montreal-ACS@state.gov
For case-specific inquiries for immigrant, fiancé(e), "V", and diversity
visa lottery cases, email: Montreal-IV/DV@state.gov
For non-immigrant visa inquiries that are not appointment-related,
email: Montreal-NIV@state.gov

Embassy Ottawa
Consular Section, United States Embassy
490 Sussex Drive
Mailing Address:
PO Box 866, Station B
Ottawa, Ontario K1P 5T1

Consulate General Québec
2 Place Terrasse Dufferin
Mailing Address:
B.P. 939, Québec
Québec G1R 4T9

Consulate General Toronto
360 University Avenue
Toronto, Ontario, M5G 1S4
www.usconsulatetoronto.ca

Consulate General Vancouver
1075 West Pender Street, Mezzanine.
Mailing address:
1095 West Pender Street
Vancouver, B.C. V6E 2M6
E-mail addresses:
Case specific visa inquiries: vancouverNIV@state.gov
Fiancée visa inquiries: vancouverK@state.gov
Passport and citizenship inquiries: vancouverACS@state.gov

Consulate General Winnipeg
Address: 860-201 Portage Avenue
Winnipeg, Manitoba R3B 3K6
www.usconsulatewinnipeg.ca

APPENDIX I: A GUIDE TO MEXICAN ROAD SIGNS   (Provided by www.tomzap.com)

In Mexico, the shapes of the different types of road signs are similar to those found in the United States and Canada. Caution signs are conventional diamond-shaped yellow signs. Stop signs are octagonal and red. White on blue signs indicate services ahead such as restaurants, hospitals, etc.

A driver will find road signs in good repair on toll roads, divided highways, and near large cities. In rural areas a driver may find signs where the color and lettering on a sign are faded and the shape or color may deviate fron the standard.

Below are some common words and phrases used in road signs. The English translation follows the Spanish word.

Alto: Stop

Autopista: Toll road or expressway. These are called Cuotas by Mexican truck drivers.

Cada el paso: Yield right of way

Circulacion (with single arrow): One-way traffic

Conceda cambio de luces: Dim your lights for oncoming traffic

Conserve su derecha: Keep to the right

Cruce de escolares: School crossing

Crucero peligro: Dangerous intersection

Curva peligrosa: Dangerous curve

Desviacion: Detour

Disminuya su velocidad: Reduce your speed

Doble circulacion: Two-way traffic

No deje piedras sobre el pavimento: Don't leave rocks on the pavement

No rebase: Don't pass

No rebase con raya continua: Do not pass where there is a solid line

No tire basura: Do not throw trash

Obedias las senales: Obey the signs

Parada: Bus stop

Puente en construction: Bridge under constriction

Tope: Speed bump

Tramo en reparacion: Section under construction

Transito lento carril derecho: Slow traffic, use the right lane

Vado: Dip

Below are more Spanish words related to driving, along with their English translations.

La puente: Bridge

El tapon de trafico: Congestion

La construccion: Construction

La direccion: Direction

El centro: Downtown

El intercambio: Interchange

La faja: Lane

La salida de autopista: Off-ramp

Le entrada de autopista: On-ramp

La estacionamiente: Parking lot

La ferrocarril: Railway

El derecho de paso: Right-of-way

El camino or la carretera: Road

La ruta: Route

El hombro de carretera: Shoulder

La velocidad: Speed

La calle: Street

El trafico: Traffic

APPENDIX J: FOOD AND OTHER NECESSITIES
IN MEXICO (with Pronunciation Guide)

Name	Pronunciation	Description
Al Lado	Awl-LAH-dough	On the side
Cabrito	Cah-Bree-toh	Young goat
Caldo	CAWL-doh	Clear soup
Carne de Res	KAR-nay Day RES	Beef
Chilaquiles	Cheel-ah-Keel-ez	Eggs, beans, tortilla strips, cheese, and peas
Chorizo	Cho-Reez-oh	Spicy and greasy sausage, may be very hot
Dulce	DOOL-say	Dessert, custard
Ensalada	En-sah-LAH-dah	Salad
Fideos	Fee-DAY-ohs	Noodles
Frijoles Refritos	Free-HOLE-es Rah-FREE-tohs	Refried beans
Huevos Fritos	Way-vos FREE-tohs	Eggs fried
Huevos Mexicana	WAY-vohs Meh-hee CAHN-ah	Same as above without tortilla
Huevos Rancheros	Way-vohs Ron-CHAIR-ohs	Eggs, fried with spicy tomato sauce on a tortilla
Huevos Revueltos	Way-vos all Rev-WELL-tohs	Eggs, scrambled
Jamon	Ha-MOAN	Thin slice of pressed ham
Jugo de Naranja	HOO-go Day Nah-RAWN-hah	Orange juice
Omlet de Queso	Ohm-LET day Kay-so	Omlet filled with melted cheese
Pan Tostada	PAWN-Toe-STAH-dah	Bread toasted
Papas Rayadas	PAH-pas-ray-AH-dahs	Hash-brown potatoes
Papas	PAH-pas	Potatoes
Pescado	Peh-SKA-doh	Fish
Pollo	POY-yoh	Chicken
Sopa de Arroz	SOAP-ah Day Ah-ROSE	Steamed rice
Tocino	Toe-SEE-noh	Sliced Bacon
Tortilla de Harina	Tor-TEE-yah Day Ah-REEN-nah	Tortilla made from flour
Tortilla de Maize	Tor-TEE-yah Day Mah-EEZE	Tortilla made from corn
Venduras	Var-DUR-ahs	General term for all vegetables

APPENDIX K: GLOSSARY OF TRANSPORTATION TERMS

49 CFR Part 166: specifications for hazardous materials that require special equipment or protection.

5-axle, Removable Gooseneck, Low Detachable, Two Axle Dolly: a low bed frame with three rear trailer axles. A two-axle dolly is attached to the rear of the trailer.

Accident Packet: given by most companies to drivers to help them handle their responsibilities at the scene of an accident. Packets usually contain basic instructions for handling the scene of an accident, a preliminary accident report or memo, and witness cards.

Ad Valorem: "according to value." A percentage charge, tax, or duty applied to a product or service.

Affiliate: a business located in one country that is at least 10 percent or more directly or indirectly owned or controlled by a person of another country.

Agent: a person or company that acts as the official representative of another, such as a consignee's agent.

Agent/Distributor Service (ADS): fee-based service that locates foreign import agents and distributors for exporters.

Antidumping Duty: a duty on import goods that is the result of an antidumping order.

Antidumping Laws: laws to combat or stop dumping.

Antidumping Petition: petition filed by a United States industry, alleging that foreign goods are being sold in the United States at "less than fair value" and threatening United States industry.

Arrester Beds: an escape ramp made of loose material, usually pea gravel, 300 to 700 feet long.

Articulation: movement between two separate parts, such as a tractor and a trailer.

Atlas: collection of maps of states, major cities, and areas. Some atlases may also include the location of permanent scales, low underpasses, size and weight limits, fuel taxes, designated routes, and state laws for access to the designated highway system.

Automated Export Reporting Program (AERP): allows for electronic submission of most information on the Shipper's Export Declaration.

Bail-out Area: places you can use to avoid a crash.

Bill of Lading (B/L): this document is one you should not leave without. You should have a B/L for each shipment in your load that describes in detail each shipment on your truck.

Blood Alcohol Content (BAC): the amount of alcohol in the bloodstream that determines the level of intoxication.

Cab: the part of the vehicle where the driver sits. Keep it clean so that papers and trash do not obstruct your view or fall under the clutch, brake, or accelerator.

Canada/United States Transit Manifest (A8B/7512B): an interchangeable form that is used for importing United States goods or Canadian goods moving through the United States then back to Canada.

Canadian Waste Manifest: If any of your shipments contains hazardous wastes, you must give photocopies of the Canadian Waste Manifest to Canada Customs, along with a "Notice/Transit Notice" form and a letter to proceed, or a written confirmation letter. Make sure you always keep the original for the extent of your trip and give photocopies to Customs.

Cargo Control Document (CCD) (A8A or A8A (B): this is the carrier's report to Customs. It is either the carrier's or driver's responsibility to complete.

Cargo Doors: doors at the back or side of a trailer where cargo may be loaded or unloaded. All hinges should be secure and rust and damage free.

Cargo Securement Devices: tie-downs, chains, tarps, and other methods of securing cargo in flatbeds. During inspection, make sure there is no damage and that the devices can withstand 1 1/2 times the amount of pressure from the load.

Carnets: documents from customs to allow an importer to send samples without paying duties or posting bonds.

Carrier: an organization that hauls cargo by truck.

Carrier's Time Record: a record maintained by the carrier that records a driver's duty status.

Cash Against Documents: when a bill of lading is presented, payment is made.

Center of Gravity: the point where weight acts as a force. Center of gravity affects the vehicle's stability.

Centers for Disease Control (CDC): agency to notify if a cargo spill contains a disease-causing agent.

Certificate of Export (E15): If any of the shipments you are carrying need to be examined prior to their departure from Canada, they must be presented to Customs for certification along with an E15 document.

Certificate of Inspection: certifies that the goods, usually perishable items, were in good condition at the time of shipment.

Certificate of Origin: a signed certificate that states the origin of the exported items.

Certificate of Registration (4455): also known as Customs Form 4455, the certificate is required on NAFTA shipment for goods exempt from duty under the Harmonized Tariff Schedule of the United States Customs Form 4455 serves as an application for this exemption when accompanied by the appropriate inventory.

Checklist: a list of parts of the vehicle to check or inspect.

Chemical Transportation Emergency Center (CHEMTREC): tells emergency personnel what they need to know to take care of a chemical problem. It also helps make the proper notifications and supplies the emergency personnel with expert technical assistance.

Class A Fire: a fire in ordinary combustibles such as wood, paper, and cloth.

Class B Fire: a fire in flammable or combustible liquids and gases such as gasoline, diesel fuel, alcohol, paint, acetylene, hydrogen.

Class C Fire: a fire in live electrical equipment. You must put it out with something that does not conduct electricity. After the electricity is cut off, extinguishers suitable for Class A or Class B fires may be used.

Class D Fire: a fire in combustible metals such as magnesium and sodium. These fires can only be put out with special chemicals or powders.

COD Shipments: shipments in which the driver Collects payment On Delivery for freight, or cargo and freight.

Collection Papers: invoices, bills of lading, purchase orders, etc. submitted to a purchaser for the purpose of payment.

Combination Vehicle: when you add a trailer to a tractor or a straight truck. It is also called a combination rig.

Combined Axle Weight: the load of all axles (tandem or triple axles).

Commercial Driver's License (CDL): required for operating commercial motorized vehicles.

Commercial Vehicle Safety Act of 1986 (CMVSA/86): law passed to make sure all CMV drivers were qualified.

Common Carrier: a motor carrier that offers its services to all individuals and businesses.

Communication: telling other drivers what you are going to do.

Coupling: joining a tractor to a trailer.

Coupling Device: a device called a converter gear or dolly that makes it possible to attach one trailer to another or to a tractor.

CPR: (cardiopulmonary resuscitation).

Customer Relations: how you, as a truck driver, get along with customers.

Customhouse or Customs Broker (CHB): licensed by the United States Customs Service to transact customs business for others.

Customs Service's Automated Commercial System (ACS): a computerized data processing center that links customhouses, members of the import trade community, and other government agencies with Customs computer.

Dead Axle: an axle that is not powered.

Defensive Driving: driving in a manner to avoid or get out of problems that may be created by other drivers.

Deliver, or Terminal, Carrier: the carrier that delivers the shipment to the consignee.

Delivery Receipt: a paper signed by the consignee or an agent of the consignee accepting the shipment from the driver. The driver keeps the receipt as proof of delivery.

Department of Motor Vehicles (DMV): assists in making state laws and regulations for motor carriers.

Department of Transportation (DOT): administers federal regulations and interstate trucking operations.

Detention Time or Demurrage: detaining a vehicle beyond a given time. Payment is made to the carrier when delivery is delayed by the shipper.

Documentation: paperwork that accompanies shipments and provides an accurate record of the cargo. In some cases, it also serves as a contract for the transportation services.

Driver's Daily Log or Driver's Log: the most commonly used record of duty status for drivers.

Driving Time: all time spent at the controls of the rig. Written as a (D) on the log book.

Dumping: the sale of goods in a foreign market for less than fair value.

Duty: tax on imports.

Emergency Equipment: equipment needed during an emergency. For a CMV, the emergency equipment consists of a fire extinguisher, reflective emergency triangles, fuses if needed, tire change kit, accident notification kit, and a list of emergency numbers. It is also a good option to have extra food, drinking water, medicine, extra clothes, and cold weather outerwear.

Emergency Relay Valve: relays air from the trailer air tank to the brake chambers. If there is a break in the lines between the tractor and trailer, the valve sends air from the trailer reservoir to the brake chambers.

Emergency Stopping: stopping quickly while keeping the vehicle under control.

Emergency Triangles: reflective triangles to be carried on all current commercial vehicles and required by law under FMCSR 393.95.

Employer-Employee Relations: how you, as a truck driver, get along with your employer, the carrier.

En-route Inspection: a rig's control and instrument check while driving and a check of critical items at each stop.

Environmental Protection Agency (EPA): regulates hazardous materials.

Escape Ramps: areas used to stop runaway rigs by either sinking the rig in loose gravel or sand or sending it up an incline. They are designed to stop a vehicle safely without injuring people or damaging the cargo.

Exempt Commodity Broker: a broker who handles commodities for shipment that are exempted from federal regulation, such as agricultural or forestry products.

Export Broker: matches importers with buyers for a fee, but does not take part in the actual sales transaction.

Export Declaration (B13 or B13A): only necessary for goods you are carrying that will leave Canada.

Exporter's Certificate of Origin: the document that certifies the origin of goods for preferential rate of duty or tax. Article 502 of the NAFTA requires that an importer base his claims on the exporter's written certificate of origin. This may be the United States-approved CF 434, CERTIFICATE OF ORIGIN; the Canadian Certificate of Origin (Canadian Form B-232); or the Mexican Certificate of Origin (Certificado de Origen). This certificate may cover a single shipment or may be utilized as a blanket declaration for a period of 12 months. In either case, the certificate must be in the importer's possession when making the claim.

Fatigue: being very tired from overwork, stress, or lack of sleep.

Federal Bridge Formula: a formula used to figure permissible gross loads. It also requires minimum distances between the tractor and trailer axles.

Federal Form MCS-150: a form used by the FMCSA to collect general identification data from motor carriers.

Federal Form MCS-151 (Part A): the first page of the Safety/ Compliance Review. It provides identifying data about the motor carrier (i.e., name, address, number of trucks, etc.).

Federal Motor Carrier Safety Regulations (FMCSR): federal laws that regulate commercial vehicle operation.

Federal Regulations for Hazardous Materials Transport: federal laws that regulate the manner in which hazardous materials must be shipped.

Fire Extinguishers: used to put out fires; they are usually marked by a letter and symbol to indicate the classes of fires for which they can be used. Every truck or truck-tractor with a gross vehicle weight rating (GVRW) of 10,001 pounds or more must have a fire extinguisher.

First Aid: immediate and temporary care given to a victim until professional help arrives.

Fixed or Stationary Trailer Tandem Axle Assembly: a tandem axle that is placed to get the best weight distribution between the tractor and the trailer, but cannot be moved. Weight adjustments between the tractor and the trailer are then made by moving, or shifting, the load inside the trailer.

Fixed-Mount Fifth Wheel: the fifth wheel that is secured in a fixed position behind the cab.

FMCSR 392.4: regulation prohibiting driving while under the influence of any dangerous drug. These drugs include: narcotics, morphine, heroin, codeine, and amphetamines.

FMCSR, Section 392.9: the part of the federal law that protects the driver by prohibiting driving a truck that is not loaded or secured properly.

FMCSR, Part 396, Inspection, Repair, and Maintenance of Motor Vehicles: where you can find out-of-service regulations. By law you must know the requirements of FMCSR 396.9 (c), Motor Vehicle Declared Out-of-Service.

FMCSR 397: regulations that deal with driving and parking vehicles with hazardous materials.

FMCSR 397.3: requires all vehicles carrying hazardous materials to comply with state and local restrictions on routes and parking.

FMCSR 397.5: the safe haven regulation that requires all vehicles carrying Class A or Class B explosives (Explosives 1.1 through 1.3) to be attended at all times.

FMCSR 397.9: controls the routes of hazmat carriers. Trips must be planned in the best interest of public safety.

For-Hire Carrier: an organization that has as its primary business hauling cargo by truck.

Forklift: used for loading pallets and heavy objects.

Freight Bills: bills prepared by the carrier from the Bill of Lading that must be signed by the consignee before the cargo can be unloaded and indicate whether the charges are prepaid or COD.

Freight Broker: a person or company that arranges for transporting freight.

Freight Forwarder: a person who gathers small shipments from various shippers and puts them together into larger shipments. These shipments then may go to a break-bulk facility where they are broken down for delivery to the consignees.

General Knowledge Test: the written test all CDL applicants must take to see how much they know about the laws regulating the trucking industry.

Gross Combination Vehicle Weight Rating (GCWR): the total weight of a tractor, trailer, and load.

Gross Vehicle Weight (GVW): the total weight of a straight truck and load.

Gross Vehicle Weight Rating (GVWR): the total weight of a tractor and all trailers.

Hand Truck: used to carry small loads from the trailer to a storage area.

Hazard: Any road condition or road user (driver, cyclist, pedestrian, or animal) that presents a possible danger to you or your rig.

Hazardous Material: Material that may pose a risk to health, safety, and property while being transported.

Hazardous Material Shipping Papers: required for each shipment, listing each item by the proper shipping name, hazard class, identification number, and packing group.

Hazardous Materials Endorsement: an endorsement on a CDL that all drivers who transport hazardous material must obtain.

Hazardous Materials Incident Report: a written report that must be filed within 15 days if there is an unintended release of hazardous materials.

Hazardous Materials Regulations: standards set by the Research and Special Programs Administration (RSPA) Office of Hazardous Materials Transportation (OHMT) that regulates how hazardous materials are shipped.

Hazardous Materials Shipping Paper: a Bill of Lading that describes hazardous materials by the proper shipping name, hazard class, identification number, and the quantity being shipped. This form must be legible.

Hazardous Waste Manifest: A form (EPA-8700-22) that describes hazardous waste and identifies the shipper, carrier, and destination by name and by the identification numbers assigned by the Environmental Protection Agency. The shipper prepares, dates, and signs the Manifest. All carriers of the shipment must sign the paper. It must also be signed by the consignee. The driver keeps a copy.

Hazmat Labels: labels resembling small placards that are placed on packages near the proper shipping name and identification number.

Helper Service: a helper is to be provided for loading or unloading freight. The Bill of Lading specifies who will pay for the helper.

HMR 177.810: requires drivers of vehicles containing hazardous materials to obey state and local laws for the use of tunnels.

Hours of Service: the amount of time you may spend on duty.

Household Goods Bill of Lading: used by moving companies for their shipments. This type of bill serves as a legal contract between the shipper and the carrier.

Identification (ID) Number: four-digit numbers used to identify all hazardous materials.

Idling: letting the engine run while the rig is not moving.

Individual Wheel Weight: the load each wheel is supporting. It is usually checked by a state or local official with a portable scale.

Inner Bridge: the distance between the center of the rearmost tractor axle and the center of the leading trailer axle. Determines weight limits.

Inside Delivery: indicates the freight is to be delivered inside instead of unloaded at the curb.

Inspection Routine: list of steps you go through to inspect your vehicle in the same way so that you do not forget a step.

International Registration Plan (IRP): an agreement among the states and Canadian provinces for paying registration fees that are based on the percentage of miles operated in each state or province.

Interstate: between states.

Interstate Operating Authority: issued by the DOT.

Interstate Routes: these routes have separate opposing traffic, have limited access, and bypass many small communities.

Intrastate: within the state.

Invoice: a bill from the shipper that lists the goods, prices, and total due. This may be mailed to the consignee, or the driver may have to give it to the consignee if it is a COD shipment.

Irregular Route: an irregular route describes long-distance transport between a combination of origin and destination points using any suitable route.

IT Bond: subject to Customs Inspection and Permit. If you are planning to clear your load inland, your trailer is not sealed, or you are moving goods in-bond, you will need either one or both a 7512 and a 7512C.

Just in Time (JIT) Delivery System: a method of shipping that gets rid of the costly overhead of warehousing stock.

Labels: labels for hazard class look very much like small placards and should be placed near the proper shipping name and identification number.

Landing Gear: on a trailer, used to support the load while it is not under a tractor.

Livestock Transport Trailer: these trailers are either flat floor or double drop frame design. They are used to carry live animals.

Local Pickup and Delivery: the driver operates in and around cities. He or she will usually be delivering freight to its final destination.

Local Truck Routes: many cities and towns have designated routes for trucks.

Long-Distance Transport: cargo is transported from a point of origin to one or more distant destinations.

Maintenance Policy: guidelines companies set up that tell drivers and mechanics what their responsibilities are in servicing and maintaining their vehicles.

Malfunction: when a part of a system does not work properly.

Managing Your Speed: adjusting your speed for the road, weather, and traffic conditions.

Meet and Turn: a type of relay run in which two drivers start toward each other from different points and meet at a chosen mid-point. At the meeting place, the drivers exchange complete units or only trailers. Then each driver goes back to his or her starting point.

Motor Carrier/Carrier: the person or company that is in the business of transporting goods.

NAFTA Certificate of Origin: importers must provide Canadian Customs with a NAFTA Certificate of Origin for goods that qualify as originating under the North American Free Trade Agreement.

National Network: roadways that allow truck combinations to operate.

National Response Center: helps coordinate the emergency forces in response to major chemical hazards.

National System of Interstate Highways: also known as the Designated System or National Network. Consists of the Interstates and many additional multi-lane, divided highways, such as the United States routes.

North American Free Trade Agreement (NAFTA): a free trade agreement between Canada, the United States, and Mexico to reduce tarrifs or eliminate them altogether for goods imported into these countries.

Nuclear Regulatory Commission (NRC): regulates hazardous materials.

Occupational Safety and Health Administration (OSHA): the mission of OSHA is to save lives, prevent injuries and protect the health of America's workers.

Off-duty Time (OFF): any time during which the driver is relieved of all on-duty time responsibilities.

Office of Hazardous Materials Transportation (OHMT): part of the Research and Special Programs Administration (RSPA) that classifies hazardous materials.

Office of Motor Carriers (OMC): part of the Federal Highway Administration (FHWA) that issues and enforces the Federal Motor Carrier Safety Regulations.

On-duty Time (ON): the time the driver begins work, or must be ready to go to work, until the time he or she is relieved from work of any kind.

Open Dispatch: the driver goes from the point of origin to a distant point.

Order Notify Bill of Lading: a bill of lading that permits the shipper to collect payment before the shipment reaches the destination. The driver must pick up the consignee's copy of the Bill of Lading before he or she delivers the shipment.

Order Notify Shipment: one in which payment for the goods is made when the driver gets a copy of the Order Notify Bill of Lading from the consignee.

Originating, or Pickup, Carrier: the carrier that first accepts the shipment from the shipper.

Over-the-Counter Drugs: drugs that don't need a prescription. Note: These drugs may still have a side effect (like drowsiness) that you should be aware of.

Over-the-Road: cargo that is hauled on regular routes. Drivers may be away for a week or more.

Overweight Load: cargo that weighs more than the legal limit permits.

Overwidth Load: cargo that is wider than the legal limit permits.

Packing Slip: a detailed list of packed goods that is prepared by the shipper.

Placards: 10 3/4-inch square and turned upright on a point in a diamond shape. Federal laws specify when placards must be displayed on vehicles transporting hazardous materials.

Port of Entry: locations where the driver must stop and prove the carrier has authority to operate in the state.

Posted Bridges: many bridges have special weight restrictions. Do not cross a bridge if your rig's weight is more than the weight that is posted. Some fines are as much as $10,000.

Post-trip Inspection: a thorough check of the rig at the end of a trip.

Prepaid Shipments: ones in which the transportation charges are paid at the shipping point.

Prescription Drugs: drugs that are prescribed by a doctor.

Pre-trip Inspection: a systematic parts and system check made before each trip.

Preventive Maintenance: servicing that is done at regular intervals on a truck.

Principal Place of Business: the main office of the carrier where all records are kept.

Private Carrier: an organization that uses trucks to transport its own goods in its own trucks.

Pro Forma Invoice: a company invoice printed on official company paper to represent the sale of goods to the purchaser. Also needed for goods to be released into Canada.

Pro Numbers: preprinted numbers on freight bills that are often used to identify the freight bill.

Public Relations: how you, as a truck driver, get along with the public.

Receiver/Consignee: the person or company to whom the goods are being shipped or consigned.

Refrigerated Trailer: used for hauling cargo that needs to be refrigerated.

Regular Route: refers to line-haul transport between given origins and destinations using assigned highways.

Regular Run: the driver operates between the same points on each trip and may or may not have a regular starting and finishing time for each period of driving.

Relay Run: refers to a trip in which a driver drives and then goes off-duty as prescribed by the hours of service laws. Another driver takes the unit on to the next point. This cycle may be repeated several times as the truck is driven from origin to final destination by several different drivers.

Residential Delivery: The Bill of Lading will specify the address and method of collecting payment if the shipment is to a residence.

Restricted Routes: routes that you are not allowed to go on because the route is hazardous or prone to accidents.

Safe Haven: an area approved in writing by local, state, or federal officials in which unattended vehicles carrying Class A or Class B explosives may be parked.

Security Seals: seals placed on cargo containers by shippers that do not let the driver fully inspect the load.

Shipper's Export Declaration (7525-V): combined forms for bonded shipments moving in transit and for subsequent export. Needed for the following conditions: Entering Canada/Mexico to be stored and ultimately shipped to third countries that are not known at the time of export. Requires a United States Department of Justice Drug Enforcement Administration export declaration (21CFR, part 1313) subject to the International Traffic in Arms regulations; or requires a validated license from the United States Department of Commerce.

Sleeper Berth (SB): a berth in the tractor cab in which the driver can sleep. Its size and other specifications are determined by law.

Sleeper Berth Time: actual time spent resting in an approved type of sleeper berth.

Sleeper Operations: the driver of a rig that has a sleeper berth can accumulate the required off-duty time by using the sleeper facility.

Speed: the rate of motion of your rig.

Speeding: driving faster than the legal or posted speed limit or driving too fast for the conditions.

Speedometer: indicates road speed in miles and kilometers per hour and is required by law to work.

State Primary Routes: within each state, these are the major routes.

Storage and Delay Charges: an additional amount to be paid to the carrier if a delivery is postponed by the consignee or shipper or a shipment must be stored before it can be delivered. These terms are stated in the Bill of Lading.

Straight Bill of Lading: a contract that provides for delivery of a shipment to the consignee. The driver does not need to get a copy from the consignee when the goods are delivered.

T&E Bond: combined forms for bonded shipments that are moving in transit.

Temporary Admission Permit (E29B): necessary document if anything in your freight is being temporarily imported into Canada and later exported. For example, items that need to be repaired or used in a show or performance. A security deposit or bond, equal to the amount of duties and taxes that would be charged if the goods were to be imported, may be demanded by Canada Customs.

Test Study Books: books sold by Delmar Learning, Inc. that will help you study for and pass your CDL tests.

The National Transportation Safety Board (NTSB): investigates accidents and offers solutions to prevent future accidents.

Through Bill of Lading: a bill of lading used for shipments transported by more than one carrier that has a fixed rate for the service of all of the carriers.

Toll Roads: except for having to pay a toll, these roads are similar to the interstates.

Total Stopping Distance: the driver reaction distance plus the vehicle braking distance.

Trade Information Center: an information clearing house on federal programs to assist United States exporters. Telephone: 1-800-872-8723 (800-USA-TRADE).

Transportation Charges: fees for transportation services.

Transportation Entry and Manifest of Goods (7512): for those goods that will be exported temporarily for repair; U.S. Customs will inspect the goods on their return.

Under the Influence: refers to any driver operating under the influence of alcohol or drugs.

Uniform Straight Bill of Lading: a contract that the parties cannot change. The goods must be delivered to the consignee or an authorized representative.

United States Coast Guard National Response Center: helps coordinate emergency forces in response to chemical hazards.

United States Inward Cargo Manifest (7533): required for all imports into the United States. This form should be completed by the shipper. If none is available, one can be completed by using the Bill of Lading.

United States Numbered Routes: major through-routes. Those that parallel the Interstates may be good alternatives in case of delays on the Interstate.

Vehicle Condition Report (VCR): a daily report filed with the supervisor by each driver that states the true condition of each truck they drove that day.

Visa: a stamp on a foreigner's passport that states they can enter the country. You can have a work visa, temporary visa, etc.

Warehouse Receipt: a receipt kept by the driver to prove the shipment was unloaded at a warehouse.

Weight Distance Tax: also called a mileage tax, ton-mile tax, or axle tax. A tax paid by the carrier that is based on the annual ton mileage.

APPENDIX L: SPEED LIMITS

Speed limits as of 2001—United States Department of Transportation

State	Cars	Trucks	Comments
Alabama	70*	70*	*Interstates only. 65 on highways with 4 or more lanes; 55 on other highways.
Alaska	65*	65*	*Interstates and rural roads.
Arizona	75*	75*	*Rural Interstates only; other highways 65.
Arkansas	70*	65*	*As posted for controlled access highways only. Other roads 60 for cars, 50 for trucks.
California	70*	55	*Generally 65 on divided highways unless otherwise posted.
Colorado	75*	75*	*Generally 65 on Interstates, 55 on other highways, unless otherwise posted.
Connecticut	65*	65*	*Limited access highways; otherwise 55.
Delaware	65*	65*	*Generally 55 on 4-lane roads and divided highways unless otherwise posted.
District of Columbia	55	55	
Florida	70*	70*	*On limited access highways; 65 on divided 4-lane highways in rural areas.
Georgia	70*	70*	*Divided highways in rural areas. 65 on urban interstates and State divided highways without full access control.
Hawaii	55	55	
Idaho	75*	65	*Interstate highways; 65 on State highways.
Illinois	65*	55	*Divided highways with 4 lanes.
Indiana	65*	60*	*Rural interstates, otherwise 55.

(continued)

State	Cars	Trucks	Comments
Iowa	65*	65*	*Controlled access, multilane highways, unless otherwise posted.
Kansas	70*	70*	*Multilane highways; 65 on other State highways.
Kentucky	65*	65*	*Fully controlled access divided highways with 4 or more lanes.
Louisiana	70*	70*	*Controlled access highways; 65 on other multilane divided highways.
Maine	65*	65*	*Divided, controlled access highways.
Maryland	65*	65*	*Divided highways.
Massachusetts	65*	65*	*On certain interstates.
Michigan	70*	55	*On certain freeways; other freeways 65.
Minnesota	70*	70*	*Rural interstates; 65 on other freeways and expressways.
Mississippi	70	70	
Missouri	70*	70*	*On rural interstates and freeways; 65 on rural expressways; 60 on urban interstates, freeways and expressways.
Montana	75*	65**	*Rural interstates; 65 on urban interstates; 70 during daytime on other highways; 65 during nighttime on other highways. **Other highways 60 daytime; 55 night time.
Nebraska	75*	75*	*On freeways and interstates.
Nevada	75	75	
New Hampshire	65*	65*	*Divided highways with 4 lanes or more; 55 on other highways.
New Jersey	65*	65*	*Selected state highways; 55 on other highways.
New Mexico	75	75	
New York	65*	65*	*On certain stretches of divided highways; 55 on other highways.
North Carolina	70*	70*	*On selected controlled access highways; 55 on other highways.
North Dakota	70*	70*	*Interstates only; other divided highways: 65 daytime, 55 night time.
Ohio	65*	55	*On certain interstates and freeways; 55 on other interstates and freeways.
Oklahoma	75*	75*	*Turnpike and certain interstates; 70 on other 4-lane highways and some 2-lane highways.
Oregon	65*	55	*Rural interstates; 55 on other highways.
Pennsylvania	65*	65*	*Rural interstates and other designated freeways; 55 elsewhere.
Rhode Island	65	65	
South Carolina	70*	70*	*Interstates and other freeways; 60 on other divided primary highways.
South Dakota	75*	75*	*Interstates only; 65 on other highways.
Tennessee	70*	70*	*Interstates only; 65 on other limited access highways.

State	Cars	Trucks	Comments
Texas	70*	70*	*Daytime on U.S. and state highways in rural areas; 65 during night time.
Utah	75*	75*	*Limited access highways; otherwise 65.
Vermont	65*	65*	*Certain controlled access highways.
Virginia	65*	65*	*Rural limited-access highways; 55 on other highways.
Washington	70	60	
West Virginia	70*	70*	*Interstates only; 65 on other highways.
Wisconsin	65	65	
Wyoming	75*	75*	*Interstates only; 65 on other highways.

Please use care as this information changes frequently. We cannot guarantee the accuracy or timeliness of what has been reported to ATA.

Always observe the POSTED limit.

Einstein discovers the speed of light.

Cartoon by T. McCracken.

Maximum posted speed limits for U.S. Passenger vehicles as of January 2003

Due to the variances of speed limits allowed in the 50 United States and the District of Columbia, drivers should be aware of the maximum limits in each state he or she enters. Within the United States, the interstate system is divided into urban and rural sections. An urban section represents an area population of 5,000 to 49,999. A designated urbanized area represents a population of 50,000 or greater.

State	Rural Inter-states Cars (mph)	Urban Inter-states Cars (mph)	Other Limited Access Roads Cars (mph)	Other Roads Cars (mph)	Effective Date of Limits on Rural Inter-states	Urban Inter-states	Effective Date of Limits on Other Limited Access Roads	Other Roads
Alabama	70	70	65	65	5/9/96	5/9/96	5/9/96	5/9/96
Alaska	65	55	65	55	1/15/88	no action	8/25/99	no action
Arizona	75	55	55	55	12/8/95	no action	no action	no action
Arkansas	70 trucks: 65	55	60	55	8/19/96	no action	8/19/96	no action
California	70 trucks: 55	65	70	65	1/7/96	1/7/96	1/7/96	no action
Colorado	75	65	65	65	6/24/96	6/24/96	6/24/96	no action
Connecticut	65	55	65	55	10/1/98	no action	10/1/98	no action
Delaware	65	55	65	55	1/17/96	no action	1/17/96	no action
District of Columbia	N/A	55	N/A	25	1974	no action	no action	no action
Florida	70	65	70	65	4/8/96	4/8/96	4/8/96	4/8/96
Georgia	70	65	65	65	7/1/96	7/1/96	7/1/96	7/1/96
Hawaii	60	50	45	45	1974	no action	no action	no action
Idaho	75 trucks: 65	65	65	65	5/1/96	5/1/96	5/1/96	5/1/96
Illinois	65 trucks: 55	55	65	55	4/27/87	no action	1/25/96	no action
Indiana	65 trucks: 60	55	55	55	6/1/87	no action	no action	no action
Iowa	65	55	65	55	5/12/87	no action	6/6/96	no action
Kansas	70	70	70	65	3/7/96	3/7/96	3/7/96	3/7/96
Kentucky	65	55	55	55	6/8/87	no action	no action	no action
Louisiana	70	55	70	65	8/15/97	no action	8/15/97	8/15/97

State	Rural Inter-states Cars (mph)	Urban Inter-states Cars (mph)	Other Limited Access Roads Cars (mph)	Other Roads Cars (mph)	Effective Date of Limits on Rural Inter-states	Urban Inter-states	Effective Date of Limits on Other Limited Access Roads	Other Roads
Maine	65	55	55	55	6/12/87	no action	no action	no action
Maryland	65	65	65	55	7/1/95	8/1/96	8/1/96	no action
Massachusetts	65	65	65	55	1/5/92	1/29/96	1/29/96	no action
Michigan	70 trucks: 55	65	70	55	8/1/96	8/1/96	8/1/96	no action
Minnesota	70	65	65	55	7/1/97	7/1/97	7/1/97	no action
Mississippi	70	70	70	65	2/29/96	2/29/96	2/29/96	2/29/96
Missouri	70	60	70	65	3/13/96	3/13/96	3/13/96	3/13/96
Montana	75 trucks: 65	65	day: 70 night: 65	day: 70 night: 65	5/28/99	5/28/99	5/28/99	5/28/99
Nebraska	75	65	65	60	6/1/96	6/1/96	6/1/96	6/1/96
Nevada	75	65	70	70	12/8/95	12/8/95	12/8/95	12/8/95
New Hampshire	65	65	55	55	4/16/87	5/29/96	no action	no action
New Jersey	65	55	65	55	1/19/98	no action	1/19/98	no action
New Mexico	75	55	65	55	5/15/96	no action	5/15/96	no action
New York	65	65	65	55	8/1/95	7/16/96	7/16/96	no action
North Carolina	70	65	65	55	8/5/96	8/5/96	10/1/96	no action
North Dakota	70	55	65	day: 65 night: 55	6/10/96	no action	6/10/96	6/10/96
Ohio	65 trucks: 55	65	55	55	7/15/87	7/28/96	no action	no action
Oklahoma	75	70	70	70	8/29/96	8/29/96	8/29/96	8/29/96
Oregon	65 trucks: 55	55	55	55	6/27/87	no action	no action	no action
Pennsylvania	65	55	65	55	7/13/95	no action	5/10/96	no action
Rhode Island	65	55	55	55	5/12/96	no action	no action	no action
South Carolina	70	70	60	55	4/30/99	4/30/99	4/30/99	no action
South Dakota	75	65	65	65	4/1/96	4/1/96	4/1/96	4/1/96
Tennessee	70	70	70	55	3/25/98	5/15/01	5/15/01	no action
Texas	70	70	70	70	12/8/95	12/8/95	12/8/95	12/8/95
Utah	75	65	65	65	5/1/96	5/1/96	no action	no action

(continued)

State	Rural Inter-states Cars (mph)	Urban Inter-states Cars (mph)	Other Limited Access Roads Cars (mph)	Other Roads Cars (mph)	Effective Date of Limits on Rural Inter-states	Urban Inter-states	Effective Date of Limits on Other Limited Access Roads	Other Roads
Vermont	65	55	50	50	4/21/87	no action	no action	no action
Virginia	65	55	65	55	7/1/88	no action	2/13/96	no action
Washington	70 trucks: 60	60	55	55	3/15/96	3/15/96	no action	no action
West Virginia	70	55	65	55	8/25/97	no action	8/25/97	no action
Wisconsin	65	65	65	55	6/17/87	8/1/96	8/1/96	no action
Wyoming	75	60	65	65	12/8/95	12/8/95	12/8/95	12/8/95

APPENDIX M: CONVERSION FACTORS CHART

(Conversions of metric, imperial, and United States measurement systems.)

To change	To	Multiply by
acres	hectares	.4047
acres	square feet	43,560
acres	square miles	.001562
Btu/hour	horsepower	.0003930
Btu	kilowatt-hour	.0002931
Btu/hour	watts	.2931
Bushels	cubic inches	2150.4
Bushels (U.S.)	hectoliters	.3524
centimeters	inches	.3937
centimeters	feet	.03281
cubic feet	cubic meters	.0283
cubic meters	cubic feet	35.3145
cubic meters	cubic yards	1.3079
cubic yards	cubic meters	.7646
fathom	feet	6.0

To change	To	Multiply by
feet	meters	.3048
feet	miles (nautical)	.0001645
feet	miles (statute)	.0001894
feet/second	miles/hour	.6818
furlongs	feet	660.0
furlongs	miles	.125
gallons (U.S.)	liters	3.7853
grams	pounds	.002205
hectares	acres	2.4710
hectoliters	bushels (U.S.)	2.8378
horsepower	watts	745.7
horsepower	Btu/hour	2,547
hours	days	.04167
inches	millimeters	25.4000
inches	centimeters	2.5400
kilometers	miles	.6214
kilowatt-hour	Btu	3412
knots	nautical miles/hour	1.0
knots	statute miles/hour	1.151
liters	gallons (U.S.)	.2642
liters	pecks	.1135
liters	pints (dry)	1.8162
liters	pints (liquid)	2.1134
liters	quarts (dry)	.9081
liters	quarts (liquid)	1.0567
meters	feet	3.2808
meters	miles	.0006214
meters	yards	1.0936
metric tons	tons (long)	.9842
metric tons	tons (short)	1.1023

To change	To	Multiply by
miles	kilometers	1.6093
miles	feet	5280
miles (nautical)	miles (statute)	1.1516
miles (statute)	miles (nautical)	.8684
miles/hours	feet/minute	88
millimeters	inches	.0394
pints (dry)	liters	.5506
pints (liquid)	liters	.4732
pounds	ounces	16
quarts (dry)	liters	1.1012
quarts (liquid)	liters	.9463
radians	degrees	57.30
rods	meters	5.029
rods	feet	16.5
square feet	square meters	.0929
square kilometers	square miles	.3861
square meters	square feet	10.7639
square meters	square yards	1.1960
square miles	square kilometers	2.5900
square yards	square meters	.8361
tons (long)	metric tons	1.016
tons (short)	metric tons	.9072
tons (long)	pounds	2240
tons (short)	pounds	2000
watts	Btu/hour	3.4121
watts	horsepower	.001341
yards	meters	.9144
yards	miles	.0005682

Index

reporting an emergency, 60
safety regulations, 59
vehicle safety standards, 60
United States-Canada Smart Border Declaration,
    5
United States Customs forms, 89–91
United States Department of Transportation (DOT)
    number, 53
    Research and Special Programs Administration,
        68, 71

security requirements for Canadian truck
    operators, 82

Vehicle registration, Canada, by province, 16–17
Visual search, 87–88

Wireless phones, 81
World Trade Center, 74

Yellow card, 10